Despite its serious fo___, ____ __ _ __tally upbeat book that offers positive, workable no-cost or low-cost solutions. The biggest expense will be in time, effort, caring and compassion for America's workforce as human beings, rather than inanimate "things" to be used up, thrown away and forgotten about when they are no longer useful.

Barbara Martin optimistically believes Corporate America will rise to the challenge and set new standards of corporate and human responsibility. She believes that enlightened companies can and will be motivated to use their know-how to help employees take advantage of America's countless wealth-building opportunities.

About the Author

Barbara Martin is a graduate of Rutgers University and is a licensed pharmacist practicing in California.

This book is a result of her first-hand experience in dealing with people of all ages, but particularly, seniors and young workers. Working for a large corporation, she is aware of the latent positive power that a business of any size can exert for the benefit of employees and society.

Barbara Martin knows there is a better way to face retirement. She would like to see all workers, not just highly paid managers and executives, encouraged and helped to realize their dreams of security and the good life that is possible through financial abundance.

Minimum Wage
To
Maximum
Wealth

By

Barbara Martin

Tangible Assets Publications
P.O. Box 6099
Oceanside, CA 92056

Copyright © 1990 by Tangible Assets Publications

Library of Congress Catalog Number: 88-051573

ISBN 0-9621499-6-9 (Paperback)

ISBN 0-9621499-7-7 (Hardcover)

Single copies and volume quantities may be ordered directly from the publisher. Please write for current terms and prices. Tangible Assets Publications, Mail Order Division, P.O. Box 6099, Oceanside, CA 92056.

Cover design by Robert Howard

Contents

Dedication

This book is dedicated to everyone who dreams of financial abundance. But in particular, it is for *you* if one or more of the following conditions apply:

. . . You have at least 20 years left to work and you are trapped in our society's devastating "work, spend, and up-to-the-elbows-in-debt" ethic. You are serious about the state of your financial condition but despair of ever having much more than you have right now;

. . . You are intelligent, willing and able to learn but possibly handicapped by an inadequate education (even though perhaps having a college diploma!) that tends to keep you locked into a low to moderate income track;

. . . You need and are ready to listen to some tough, common sense plain talk to make you aware of what should and can be done to improve your financial destiny;

. . . You are willing and anxious to develop the grit, guts, and pitbull determination that is necessary to get you where you want to be when you are no longer able to punch a time clock.

. . . You are ready to prove to yourself and the world that you are more than a winner; you are a miracle-maker!

Foreword

This is a book about getting your financial priorities straight. Those who are open to its basic tenets could find that it can change their financial destiny. It offers sound principles of acquiring money, keeping money and making money earn even more.

Barbara Martin makes the reader look at the facts. At retirement, many of us will spend a decade or even more, without "earned" income. Realistically, you have to rule out external financial support from any source, including Social Security. So how will you live? How will you pay for not only normal living expenses but for the increased medical care which nature dictates you will need? Project yourself into the future. No miracles will happen between now and then.

To make the matter even more urgent, the situation could get much worse. On a relative scale, current financial conditions are very strong right now. The study of cycles teaches us that in the future, maybe sometime during our lifetime, the economic environment will be much closer to that of the Great Depression. We must look at this possibility and realize that *now* is the time to insure that we are saving, minimizing debt and properly investing as much as possible.

Everyday I work with intelligent investors who have learned these lessons well. I am fortunate to have clients all across America and from all age groups and walks of life. From my interaction with them, I have learned that the people who have the large sums of money to invest and protect from taxes aren't just the doctors, lawyers and corporate presidents. My wealthiest clients are common people with common sense: blueberry farmers, chicken ranchers, Fotomat operators. Most started small, with only their own labor and eventually their savings working for them. It wasn't inheritance, it wasn't the lottery. It was working hard, working smart, and a commitment to long-term savings.

Successful investors, such as these, invest by the basics. For instance, imagine for a moment that your personal wealth is like a bathtub. There is water coming in from the faucet (income) and water going out the drain at the bottom of the tub (expenditures). There are only two ways to fill the tub: one is to open up the faucet and pour more water in and the other is to adjust the drain so that less water flows out.

Many "rags to riches" books concentrate on how to earn more income, or turn the faucet on. This book concentrates on what you can do *now* with what you have control over, your expenditures. It will teach you not only how to slow the outflow but give you sound ideas on how to invest what you have.

When you do find the money, there are sound investments which can help you achieve your financial objective. Don't look for the "get rich quick" schemes; they simply don't work. Avoid the money gurus who tell you not to ask questions but to simply follow their plan. Look for sound, guaranteed to very low risk ways to have your money work for you. It's time, and the magic power of compounding which over the years will make a significant difference in your personal net worth. And all things being equal, invest your money where it won't be eroded by annual taxation. Because even if you're in a low income tax bracket, the only thing more powerful than the power of compounding is the tax-protected power of compounding. Many innovative consumer-oriented investment plans have been created to maximize long-term savings. Examples are: single premium life, tax-deferred annuities and tax-protected life insurance plans which will pay the death benefit *to the insured* in the event of a long-term health care need.

The ironic thing about "How-To" books is that many of the people who need them most, do not read them. As you read this book, people you know will come to mind who need to learn how to save and invest money. Share this book with them. This book offers those who are ambitious for financial success an insight which will aid them to acquire money, to keep the money they earn and to make their savings earn even more.

Investing doesn't have to be a chore. It can be a rewarding hobby.

Tina K. Baughman
President
Independent Advantage Financial & Insurance Services, Inc.
Los Angeles, California

In the beginning . . .
There was awareness . . .
Followed by anger . . .
Which became the determination to
expose and correct some of the insidious
assorted injustices that we all endure
because "that's the way the system works" or
"this is the way it's always been done."
But so what if it's "written in concrete"?
Each and every one of us has the capacity
to move mountains. We just have to pick
the mountains we want to move, and
muster the will to do it.
To turn on the mental switch that will
fire up that determination may take a
verbal swift kick in the britches. So, brothers
and sisters, prepare! Your switch is about to
be swatted!

▸1◂

The Not
So Great
Awakening

If your financial situation could be described as a constant losing battle to stay two jumps ahead of bill collectors; or maybe it's just a struggle to make it from one paycheck to the next, and it *really* bothers you; or you've given up your dream of having a whole lot more than you have right now, then this book is for you. *I want it to change your life.* I truly believe that it can change your life because not only will it give you a fresh perspective about your worth as a worker and a human being, but it will give you some new ways to think about handling your income that could enable you to achieve some financial miracles.

A year ago such other-oriented, altruistic thinking would not have occurred to me. But then I went back to work and became part of the "real world" once again. I've found it's a far different world than when I last earned a paycheck -- it's a world filled with a tremendous amount of financial heartache for an awful lot of good, hard-working people.

It doesn't have to be that way.

But I'm getting ahead of things. Let me start at the "beginning."

After having been retired from the practice of Pharmacy for a number of years, I decided it was time to start carrying some of our family's financial burden. But it wasn't just that. I also needed to prove to myself that I could be self-supporting in the event of my dear husband's premature demise. You see, I am convinced his job is killing him.

He, too, is a pharmacist, employed by a large drugstore chain. At his request he had transferred to a new store closer to the ocean so that we could more easily combine work and pleasure. He did a lot of complaining about working conditions before the transfer, but it was nothing compared to what I had to listen to after the move.

On too many nights he'd drag his stressed-out body into the house and the first thing I'd hear was not a cheery "hello" but a wiped-out "This was the worst day I've ever had." If you love the guy, how often can you listen to that and not try do *something* about it?

So, needing the money, wanting to be self-sufficient and above all, determined to find out, first hand, what working conditions were *really* like, I went to work for my husband's employer. Since pharmacists are in short supply, they were happy to have me.

I rationalized that if nothing else, being in the same company and experiencing the same problems might make things easier for him. I hoped that being able to share the misery and talk about situations I could understand might defuse some of the pressure.

So, what happened?

Believe me when I tell you it's been a real learning experience, in more ways than I ever anticipated. As one co-worker put it my first day on the job, "welcome to the zoo, kiddo."

I found that "what's wrong" with the job has two sides -- some pretty stupid corporate policies and a raging bull mentality of a demanding, debt-ridden cash-poor public.

As for the company side of the problem, it didn't take long to confirm that working conditions left *much* to be desired. I now fully understand and appreciate in a way not possible before, just how severely my husband's job is grinding him into the ground. Short of quitting and perhaps "jumping from the frying pan into the fire" in another job, I don't know what we're going to do to improve the situation, but we're working on it. My sister, also a pharmacist and a long-time veteran of the corporate rat race, offered this advice: "Adjust your attitude, darling." We're trying that. But let me tell you, that approach helps only to a point. You can adjust your attitude until you are blue in the face and it doesn't change anything very much, and won't change anything significantly until corporate decision makers realize that providing decent working conditions is at least as important as raking in maximum profits. "Positive thinking" just doesn't help all that much when you have no control over antiquated management practices that include an adversarial attitude toward employees. But because we are basically "positive" people, my husband and I *do* try to "think positive" at every opportunity!

"The public" side of the problem is that many people of all ages have *severe* money problems. In some cases it's a matter of not having enough income. In other cases it's not that there isn't enough income; it's an inability to manage it. In either case the cash-poor condition very often results in abusive "taking it out on others" behavior. For example, it's part of our human nature that we don't mind spending money on things that give pleasure -- even if it means using the rent money, a credit card or borrowing from friends. But when it comes to car repairs, insurance and medical care, that's a different story. So when sickness strikes and a prescription must be filled, a lot of people enter the pharmacy with a predisposition to hate you, the pharmacist. They are already mad at God and the doctor for allowing them to get sick and mad at you because you are perceived as being in cahoots with God and the doctor to steal the money they'd rather spend in a restaurant or on a case of beer. *You are the enemy!* You control what they want and can't afford, or worse yet, you have what they need but don't want to pay for. So they vent their anger at you and *man, it is not pleasant!*

You hear a lot about consumer spending and debt but you really can't comprehend how bad it really is until you experience it at the cash register. Young teens with an allowance, older working teens, young and middle-aged workers charge or plunk down cash for the most incredible junk. It's almost as if they are responding to some intangible compelling force. And aren't they? The sophistication, intensity and relentless urging of merciless advertising that cleverly equates spending with "feeling good about yourself" is more than many people can handle. If you include peer pressure to have as much as your friends or neighbors, it's easy to see how difficult it is to stay on an even keel, let alone get ahead financially.

In essence, those are the two sides of what's wrong with the job -- the employer with antediluvian management style and the belligerent, demanding cash-poor public. But that's not the end of the story.

There's more. If it's not "news" to you, bear with me anyway because you may not have thought about it in quite the same way.

IT WON'T BE FUN FOR ANYONE

Seeing working people struggle because they don't have enough money to take care of present needs is tough. It forces you to face up to the gut-wrenching reality that the future will be even tougher -- *a lot tougher for everyone*. Frankly, it scares the daylights out of me. It's one thing to hear or read about the "hand to mouth" existence of many people, but when you have to deal with it first hand on a daily basis, it doesn't take long for the gravity of the mess to sink in. You quickly acquire a painful insight into an inevitable tragedy in the making. If you look at the picture from all angles -- the present and probable future condition of our economy; where we are headed politically, socially and morally -- it becomes clear that life in the future will be an absolutely hellish nightmare for a mind-boggling number of those working today.

There are those who might be inclined to say *So what! Let them spend themselves into poverty. We don't even know them.* In an era where "taking care of number one" has been elevated to the status of a religion, why should we be concerned about anybody else? Because if we are decent human beings, we *will* care. If that sounds too much like liberal do-goodism, then look at it from the selfish perspective that it's the *smart* thing to do. The spending excesses, the incredible "money illiteracy" (not knowing how to wisely handle the little they do have) particularly of minimally educated YUCKIES -- Young Urban Cashless Kids, the backbone of an expanding low-pay service economy -- will impact the lives and fortunes of *all of us*. They will become old -- and dependent. And God help us if we are foolish enough to believe the government will have the money to keep everybody in the style they would like. True, the government can always print more money and raise taxes, but in that case, we will all be reduced to paupers.

Is this "doom and gloom" projection an over-reaction? Hardly. This vision of the future is accurate and should be obvious to anyone who dares to look at the plight of the current crop of retirees. Sure, a lot of them are well off. But many of them -- too many -- are in dire financial straits. Many of these cash-poor seniors will argue over a dime. (*What? You want to charge me $10.85 for my prescription? I paid $10.75 for it last time. Here is my receipt to prove it!*) The irony is that today's elders are from a generation that for the most part lived modestly during their income-producing years. They put aside a "nest egg" and counted on Social Security and the company pension (if indeed there was one) to get them by in style in their final years. But in spite of such careful planning, it's not nearly enough.

Put yourself in the shoes of the infirm elderly. If you are healthy and working right now, and fairly well off financially, can you possibly imagine what it would be like to need several hundred dollars worth of medication each month to keep you free of pain or to keep your heart pumping, and not have the money or other means to pay for what you need? When you're young and healthy you don't think about that, and even if you do think about it, it's impossible to imagine what it's like. Even after hearing the panic in their voices and seeing the terror in the eyes of those who are in this horrible financial situation, it's difficult for most people without such problems to muster more than a fleeting, superficial empathy, an "isn't it too bad" reaction that is forgotten in an instant. But it doesn't change reality. All of us ought to be "sitting up and taking notice". What we are seeing today will be the future, magnified many times.

Having enough money at retirement helps prevent the onset of the "nasty, abusive old goat syndrome". It's the senior citizen version of "taking it out on others" behavior mentioned earlier. It's something that happens to too many older people, male and female. It becomes evident as a demanding, "the world owes me" demeanor that is totally repulsive. Sometimes it's brought on by sickness and pain. After all, whether you're young or old and not feeling good, it's not easy to be on your best behavior especially when things around you are not going well. But more often, abusive behavior is simply a manifestation -- a "coming into full bloom" -- of the person you've been all your life. If deep down in your soul you've been a pretty miserable human being for the past 50 years but you've gotten away with it without too many people noticing it, trust me, it will come back to haunt you. When you're young, it's easy to fake who you really are. Your vitality, good looks, cultivated charm and agile mind enable you to successfully mask the person you really are inside. But something happens to some people once they cross "the old age bridge" -- a portion of their brain seems to turn to concrete. They don't care anymore about what people think or say about them. Keeping up appearances is no longer important. It's a militant "this is the way I am and take it or leave it" attitude. The irony is, you may not care about what others think or say about you, but you will pay a price. You will be paid in kind. What you dish out you will get back. Years ago, children were taught to respect their elders, which meant putting up with odd or unkind behavior. Today, many seniors are learning they cannot expect to be treated with deference because they've reached a certain age. Young people just don't care how old you are. If you treat them like dirt that's the way they'll treat you, and then some. In the future, as more workers have less money because the government confiscates more of their earnings to take care of everybody's needs, the situation for seniors will worsen. Our young are now being primed to look favorably on a shorter life span, which means even those older people who manage to keep up a civilized demeanor when dealing with their juniors, can expect less than gracious treatment if those seniors don't have enough to pay for what they need and want.

Like it or not -- the name of the game is *money*, and above all, having plenty of it when you are no longer able to produce it by your own labor. Sure, it may not be easy to accomplish. But it's 100 percent do-able. No ifs, ands or buts.

When we are young we delude ourselves with the fantasy that *somehow*, everything will be okay. We deny that we'll get old. Or being half realistic, we acknowledge old age exists, but insist we won't have problems. Anyway, our friend, the Retirement Fairy who lives in Washington and takes dominion over the quality of our retirement years, will provide for us. *Pray that the Retirement Fairy doesn't lose his magic wand.*

THIS IS WHAT IT'S ALL ABOUT . . .

But look, why wait for the Retirement Fairy or any other kind of help that may never materialize? What ever happened to good old American self-reliance? The reality is that with just a fair amount of effort, education and motivation, a lot can be done to head off personal financial tragedy.

To that end, the basic purpose of this book is to create awareness, to do some brain-rattling consciousness raising, and above all, offer down-to-earth hope and help. It is written with an unshakable conviction that everyone who works for a living, especially those who are not self-employed, should be able to retire with substantial wealth -- with enough money to live abundantly, without pinching pennies when inflation causes higher prices for the basic necessities of life.

To help develop the thinking, motivation and action that will help set people free from the pressures and conditions that make "work and spend" money slaves of them, - - robbing them of their right to live their lives as prosperous dignified human beings, - - in the pages ahead this is what will be examined:

▶ The devastating effect of relentless media messages to *spend it all now* so that we can conform to media-manufactured images of what the "good life" should be.

▶ We'll look at what you have to give up and put up with in order to pay bills and chase that "good life" that will never be much more than a fantasy for most people.

▶　We'll look at the failure of the education system to equip people to be the best and most that they can be.

▶　We'll look at the shameful exploitation of an expanding class of service workers who work for peanuts and produce caviar profits for their "use 'em up and throw 'em away" employers.

▶　We'll look at the role of unions in a new light, particularly as it relates to helping workers become financially secure at retirement.

▶　We'll look at the financial realities and problems of old age (and yes, if you live that long, you will get old -- that's *guaranteed*).

▶　We'll look at an expert appraisal of how much money it will likely take to live comfortably in retirement.

Finally, the good news. We'll be discussing and making some basic recommendations as to what can and must be done to bring about tangible, positive changes in your life and in the life of everyone who has 20 to 30 years left to work. If enough people take seriously these recommendations and ideas and put them into action, we could see another American revolution -- a very positive revolution resulting in incredible prosperity for those who make America move -- the workers.

We all have our own perception of what it takes to be "wealthy." When you have next to nothing, $10,000 is a fortune. If you are making minimum wage, $100,000 would make you feel rich. Some would be satisfied with nothing less than a billion dollars.

For most of us, the closest we will get to wealth is watching TV or reading about how the rich live.

Another way we get close to wealth is to buy something that represents it, such as clothing bearing the name or logo of a wealthy person. But without a doubt, this is the crassest form of exploitation of the "have nots" by the "haves." Without the famous name sewn on that strategic spot, the expensive shirt or blue jeans is just another mediocre article of clothing.

We pay dearly for the privilege of serving as unpaid billboards for those who already have more money than they know what to do with, and are using our money to make even more. Which is okay, and thank God that in America enterprising folks can still make a fortune. But it's not okay unless you buy their stuff with the full understanding of what you're doing, why you're doing it and the awareness that you're being used.

2

Getting Ahead: Why Is It So Difficult?

Some people seem to be born with a built-in "money magnet." Either they have and exploit a highly marketable talent, or they develop one. Or they have exceptional business and investment skills which include using tax laws to advantage. They can't fail; regardless of what they do, it "turns to gold." But for most of us, whether or not we do well financially depends pretty much on two very basic things: (1) Our earning capacity, which is in proportion to the quality, type and level of our education (yes, there are exceptions!), and (2) What we do with what's left after the tax man takes his bite.

EDUCATION DOES
MAKE A DIFFERENCE

In days gone by, it was a lot easier to get by with a limited education. Perhaps it was easier then because even though children spent fewer years in school the quality of the teaching and what was taught was better. At least a lot of people learned to read, which made continuing self-education possible.

Today, for all the years that children spend in school, we are not as well off. Many high school graduates are poor readers and spellers and their math skills are almost non-existent. The job of teaching these basic skills has become the unwelcome burden of Corporate America. In a blistering speech delivered at the Economic Club of Detroit, October 26, 1987, the head of Xerox Corporation, David T. Kearns, accused America's schools of graduating 700,000 functional illiterates each year who can barely read their own diplomas, and letting another 700,000 more drop out. Said Kearns, "Teaching new workers basic skills is doing the schools' product recall work for them -- and frankly, I resent it."

The obvious question is, what's wrong? Contrary to what the education establishment would have us believe, the illiteracy problem is not the result of normal, average students who won't apply themselves. And it isn't "uncaring parents," either, in the majority of cases. Nor is the problem "watching too much TV," "over-crowded classrooms," or "too many learning disabled or brain damaged children."

And how about all those dropouts? Why so many? Most of them are normal kids with ordinary to very high intelligence. Believing their inability to read and perform other basic skills is their fault, which deals a crushing blow to their self-esteem, they leave and try to get a job, hoping the minimal skills they have picked up will be sufficient to help them get by in life.

Why such massive illiteracy and so many dropouts? The answer is that for the most part, schools are not using the best approach to teaching reading (and other basic skills, for that matter). And we shouldn't have to put up with this. Right now there are reading programs and teaching techniques that have proven successful for *all* children of normal intelligence, even those diagnosed as having a learning disorder called dyslexia. These programs and techniques, generally disdained by the schools, are rooted in phonics -- an approach to teaching reading that is recognized as superior by experienced reading teachers. A U.S. Department of Education booklet titled *What Works: Research About Teaching and Learning* states, "Children get a better start in reading when they are taught phonics. Learning phonics helps children understand the relationship between letters and sounds and to 'break the code' that links the words they hear with the words they see in print." But we shouldn't be surprised that phonics is not the reading method of choice. Keith Geiger, vice president of the National Education Association has said, "The No. 1 function of education is not reading, writing and arithmetic, it's learning to grow up to communicate with other people and interact with people your age." (*Los Angeles Times,* April 15, 1987). Such a shocking admission denies the reality that the use of basic skills such as reading and writing is critical for effective communication! And it also helps to explain why so many "educated" children not only can't read or write, but are also illiterate in economics, science, math, history, geography and other basics.

Being able to see but not able to read is just as much a handicap as being blind or deaf, or having just one hand or leg. You can get by in life, but it's not easy. Furthermore, the non-reader has to accept the accuracy and truth of what he *hears.* He can't go to printed sources to check things out. When it comes time to vote, either he doesn't vote at all or he casts a vote based on the hype he has seen or heard on TV, or on the uninformed opinions of friends. Which is just plain dangerous because a society with a large number of illiterates jeopardizes the freedom of *everyone.*

In addition to the illiteracy that keeps a lot of innately bright people from getting ahead, we are also plagued with a well developed educational quota system that assures an abundant supply of minimum wage workers. If you have "magnet schools" in your area, or they are being considered, then you know that "quota" has come to your community. Magnet schools are "specialty" schools that may concentrate on The Arts, Music, International Relations, Languages, Technology, College Preparation or whatever. The types of magnets established in a given area will depend on what the government determines our social and economic needs will be or should be in the future. If it is projected that doctors, dentists, engineers and the like are needed, your area may be the recipient of a magnet school that stresses college preparation or technology.

You're probably aware of the chaos that can be created by the opening of a new academic magnet school in a community. The day before registration parents will camp out all night at the school door hoping to be among the lucky ones to get their youngsters into the school. However, a magnet school obviously has limited space. It can accommodate only a certain number of desks, chairs and children. And a magnet school must take a specified number of minority students. To put it another way, "many are called but few are chosen."

There are those who would scoff at the idea that we have a quota system. If we don't have a quota system, then why are these specialty schools created? Since academic magnet schools are in such demand by parents, why can't *all* schools provide the same academic opportunities for *all* children? Why can't we have an academically superior education system, which we are paying for? The answer is "the quota system" that will provide the proper balance of low-income service workers and professionals for our increasingly government-managed society and economy. Truly, it is becoming more difficult to proclaim that we are the "masters of our own fate."

LEARNING TO ACCEPT POVERTY: DOES IT START HERE?

There is a nasty little activity going on in some classrooms that fuels the quota system. It's called the "Color Game" that supposedly teaches about racism. In praise of the program one teacher said, "Some of my kids had the American Dream idea that if you're poor you could make it to the top. I wanted to show that the people on the bottom stay on the bottom, and people on the top stay on the top." ("Color Her Gone: Teen Quits School, Sues Over 'Racism Game'", *Seattle Times*, December 2, 1987). There are countless inspiring examples of "people on the bottom" who made it to the top -- in spite of a rotten education; in spite of poverty; in spite of a broken home; in spite of anything you could think of. The tragedy is that many,

many more people could overcome their imposed handicaps and rise to the top if given enough help and encouragement.

When you think about it, such negativism and poverty peddling tends to promote the very racism and discrimination it purports to prevent. It helps keep people "in their place" to assure a ready supply of cheap labor. It also fuels the "spend it all now" syndrome. While chronic spenders are found at all economic levels, and slick advertising and spending opportunities con us all, pressure to spend is particularly compelling for those with low self-esteem, those who despair of ever having more than they have at the present moment, and those who believe they are losers.

Instead of promoting hopelessness and instilling despair, wouldn't it be more productive to use programs that show the benefits and opportunities that abound in our economic system? The irony is that a tremendous amount of excellent information and programs are available to schools and individuals. For example, in a news release dated October 25, 1988, the New York Stock Exchange announced that it has developed a series of new educational materials designed to teach students about the importance of U.S. financial markets. The materials are geared to elementary, junior and senior high classes. (Additional information available from New York Stock Exchange

Educational Products, P.O. Box 4191, Syosset, NY 11791) How many schools are taking advantage of this opportunity?

Instead of leading children to believe they can't aspire to a bountiful life, wouldn't it be wonderful if they were inspired by true accounts of real-life people who made their dreams come true? When you care about others, you don't steal their hopes and dreams for a prosperous secure future. You don't encourage them to think of themselves as losers. Rather, you will motivate them and help them acquire the skills they need to become the best and most that they can be.

The bottom line is that the kind of education you get *does* matter. For most of us, the quality of our lives in terms of economic security is *indeed* in direct proportion to the quality, type and level of our education.

The good news is that even if you've been cheated out of an education that paves the way for a prosperous future, all is not lost. It *is* possible to turn things around to your advantage if you have enough working years left. More about that later. But now, let's talk about your after-taxes income. Until you develop a "working awareness" of how your mind and emotions are yanked around to get you to part with your money, and unless you understand the need to develop a "bull dog" defensive attitude to deal with the manipulation, you will remain locked in a losing financial struggle!

AFTER TAXES: THEN WHAT HAPPENS?

What we do with our after-taxes money is a reflection of our values, goals (or lack of them), emotional stability, social conditioning and the ability to withstand peer pressure and manipulative advertising. With this in mind, let's look at some of the factors that shape the financial conditon of the American worker as well as those entering the workforce right behind him, and their prospects for future propserity. Let's start with payday.

Payday for the typical worker is like a quick trip through a revolving door. He enters with his paycheck and by the time he's made the round trip his wallet is empty. All he has to show for his 40 hours or more on the job (after he buys food, pays the rent and some of his bills) is a big fat zero. He's worked his tail off all week and there is no tangible evidence that he ever got up in the morning.

Not only is he existing from paycheck to paycheck, but he is up to his elbows in credit card debt -- balances that will take many years to reduce and may never be paid off completely. As soon as the indebtedness is reduced to a comfortable level, it's right back to the "I wanna shop 'til I drop" routine. Debt doesn't bother him too much. It's accepted as nonchalantly as a sexually transmitted disease --

"everybody's got it." He may be so happy to have "debt disease" he advertises his spending addiction with a bumper sticker on his car (which probably has 48 payments to go, and which may fall apart before it's paid for) that boasts, "When things get tough the tough go shopping." And everyone laughs and thinks it's so cute -- an unspoken agreement that *gee, we're all in the same boat, aren't we?* No, it's not cute, It's dumb. *Real dumb.*

Think about tomorrow? Five years down the road? Ten years? Retirement? *Are you kidding?*

Others have profited from all his hours on the job. *Others* have his money and they're having a *lot* of fun with it, all the way to the bank or the stock market.

"So what?" he rationalizes with a shrug. "I worked hard and I deserve some fun." Sure he does, and he *should* enjoy life. But how much "fun" is it when he's broke and he needs cash for an emergency? Borrow from friends? Lots of luck. Chances are they've been through the same revolving door.

Mindless spending is given legitimacy by regular news stories that make a connection between the health of the economy and amount of consumer activity. If folks are buying like crazy, that's supposed to be a sign that the economy is in good shape. Irrational consumer behavior may put a band-aid on the present economic situation but what will be the future "economic health" of those doing the spending today?

Another part of the problem is that most of those caught up in the "work and spend" syndrome have never been encouraged to save and invest a portion of their earnings. They've never found anyone generous enough or smart enough to give them a helping hand in getting a serious savings or investment program underway and maintained as an on-going enterprise that gives at least as much enjoyment as throwing away the discretionary portion of their paycheck (and then some) on junk they won't remember they bought the next day. Most people know nothing of the awesome power of the principle of compounding -- how even small amounts of money saved and invested regularly can become a small fortune, given time and the right rate of return. The tragic extent of such economic illiteracy was highlighted in the result of a national survey that showed more than half of all high school students could not define basic economic terms like "profit" and "inflation." ("Most Students At A Loss In Dealing With Economics," *San Diego Union*, December 29, 1988). In response to the outcome of the study sponsored by the Joint Council on Economic Education, the former chairman of the Federal Reserve Board, Paul Volker, said that students should learn such basic concepts as how wealth is created, how simple markets work, and how prices are determined. So obviously, the "economic illiteracy" is not a matter of people being "too dumb" to handle their finances, it's a matter of not being adequately educated in basic economic concepts.

Somewhere along the line we are going to have to bite the bullet and deal realistically with our economy and personal finances. Working people simply can't continue to spend to the extent that they have nothing left over to invest in their future, and expect to live and retire as dignified, independent human beings. They must be encouraged, and above all, helped to save and maintain control over at least a portion of every paycheck.

A high rate of savings makes good sense not just for individuals, but for the economy as a whole. An ample supply of money encourages business expansion and growth. It promotes the production of an abundance of goods and services, which tends to put a lid on inflation. When there is plenty to choose from in the market place it's easier to find better products at competitive prices. Certainly, there is a lot to be said for prudent money management!

And speaking of wise money management, you may be sure the wealthy aren't spending all their money on worthless trifles to shore up the economy. They are happily *investing* their money as their way of keeping the economy thriving and growing. They're *earning* money on their invested funds. These are the people who are really having a *lot* of fun! When the wealthy spend money earned from investments, some of it winds up in middle-class consumer traps, but most of their spending is done in upscale department stores or expensive "boutique" shops owned by wealthy businessmen, investors or entertainers who are always looking for ways to keep their money multiplying. The businesses along Rodeo Drive in Hollywood are a prime example of "wealth generating wealth."

Those with even more money to spend jet to Spain, Italy, France or Monaco and buy -- from entrepreneur-friends who are just as wealthy as they are -- gems, paintings, exquisitely made clothing in classic designs, and other "fun things" that retain their worth and may even grow in value over time. In other words, the super-rich tend to keep their "spending money" *in the family*. They know the manipulated masses of "have nots" will do the necessary "consumer spending" for them. The state of the economy is the least of their worries. They will have money no matter what happens to the rest of us.

ARE WE JUST PAVLOVIAN PUPPETS?

It becomes a teeny-weeny bit less difficult to hang on to your earnings if you recognize and accept the truth that a sophisticated "war" is being waged out there in the market place and the goal is to get *your* money. All of it, if possible.

You can't fight the "enemy" unless you recognize who it is and how it operates. If you stop to think about it, you soon come to the conclusion that the number one threat to your financial security is not the masked man who accosts you on a dark street and demands your wallet or the thief who breaks into your home and hauls away your stereo and other items that can be turned into cash. Those threats can often be avoided by using common sense security measures.

It is far more difficult to control "crime" when it is not perceived as such.

And it *is* a "crime" that after confiscatory taxes and government spending and misuse of *our* money, a major threat to our personal financial security is the relentless advertising that shapes our perception of what "fun" and "the good life" should be. Not only are we told what it should be, but we are not left alone until we are whipped into a buying frenzy -- willing to spend whatever it takes to get that fantasy "fun" and "the good life."

You get the impression after a while that to the advertising industry, Americans are not much more than relatives of Pavlov's dogs. You remember Pavlov, don't you? He's the Russian scientist who learned how to use bells to manipulate the behavior of dogs. He showed that if he rang a bell each time a dog was fed it would eventually salivate at the sound of the bell, even when food wasn't present. This response he termed the "conditioned reflex," a concept that has become the foundation of human behavioral psychology. As evidence of how it is used today, start watching television commercials objectively and critically to recognize their Pavlovian roots. For example, just before the "hard sell" part of a commercial, listen for a sudden sound -- a bell, laughter, a thump, a shot, -- any kind of a noise that grabs your attention and makes you look and listen. That sound sets you up to be receptive to the sales pitch that follows. Other manipulative techniques are used, but this one is the most obvious.

If a commercial is successful, the next time you are out shopping and you see the advertised item, it'll "ring a bell." Like Pavlov's dog, you'll "mentally salivate" and remember what you are supposed to do. If you don't have the cash, that's okay -- you do have a credit card, don't you? Armed with our plastic, we will not be deprived of having things we have been conditioned to want.

Pavlov also found that a dog could be conditioned to tell the difference between two bells similar in pitch, one of which meant food was coming and the other did not. If the sound of the bells was so alike that the dog could not differentiate between them, the dog developed neurotic behavior or became irritable. Does this in any way explain the often bizarre and frenetic behavior of so many people today? Are we so beset by so many bells of similar pitch and their accompanying messages to "do this" or "buy that" -- all or most of which we can't do for various reasons -- that it's making us crazy?

And of course you understand that advertising promises -- *oh, does it ever promise!* -- directly, indirectly, and subliminally -- wild parties, wanton women, sex, romance, success, sex, recognition, acceptance, sex, and still more sex if you'll just listen to the "bell" and buy the product. For example, take your typical bar scene beer commercial: A bunch of ugly, noisy super jocks with gorgeous young women hanging all over them, having the time of their lives. Just 30 seconds of "This is the good life" banter, lots of laughter and sexual innuendo is the "bell" that's going to get you to pick up that sixpack at the liquor store. At home, relaxing in your favorite chair with "the bell" still ringing in your head, you flip open the can. You can still see the bountiful beauties or the hunky dudes as you caress the cold can and guzzle the contents. For a fleeting moment you visualize yourself in that bar with all those famous and beautiful people, partying right along with them. By the time you get to the bottom of the can you are yanked back into reality and you realize that while you paid for beer, you also bought a fantasy that didn't materialize. *But hey, what the heck, the fantasy was free, so what more do you want for the price of a sixpack?* Pavlov would love it!

PEER PRESSURE, ROLE MODELS AND "OPPORTUNITIES"

When Pavlov was experimenting with his dogs, one thing he didn't have to consider was peer pressure, and the need to conform -- to be like everybody else. It can be overwhelming. We buy and wear what our friends and role models are buying and wearing. We buy what's "in." Is this year's decorating color combination pink and puce? Then, at the very least, we *must* buy new matching pink and puce towels and bed sheets. But if that's not enough, the local Cheepo Depot Home Center displays about two miles of pink and puce plastic assessories -- everything from toothbrush holders to laundry baskets to coffee mugs that are a great temptation for those who love to live in a color coordinated environment. Are clunky, grotesque shoes in style that look like they've been designed to accommodate deformed feet? Then we *must* wear them. Is orange hair that has been crimped and crinkled to the point that it looks like it was the loser in a fight with a live wire, socially accepted evidence that we're "with it"? Is underwear as outerwear a fashion statement? Never mind that it looks ridiculous and may be expensive -- we gotta wear it. If we don't, *we won't belong!* God help the loner and the non-conformist. He's *really strange. Let's not get too close to him -- we might catch what's wrong with him!* Face it: Many of us are lacking the individualism and independence that characterized our ancestors. *We seem to love being told what to think and what to do and when to do it.*

But let's not get bogged down with guilt. Not too many people make a conscious decision to be a "groupie." They are just totally unaware that acceptance of group control is instilled very early in life. From the first day we enter school, under the guise of "socialization," we are taught to find self-worth in a group, to find security and acceptance in a group, to work and play in a group, to rely on group decisions, and to be loyal to a group. Once out of school, social pressure reinforces this carefully cultivated "groupiness." As adults we still play in groups, work in groups, and rely on group decisions.

Having friends and being accepted is important, but even more important is being your own person, in control of as many elements of your life as possible.

Let's talk some more about "spending opportunities." If in fact Americans are guilty of over-consumption, as we are often said to be, are we as individuals solely responsible? Certainly not. In addition to the advertising industry we must also "thank" the industry's close cousins -- supermarkets, shopping centers, TV shopping clubs and malls. We see something advertised on TV or in the newspaper and there it is for the taking in all those inviting places.

Does anyone need to be told to stay out of the supermarket unless it's absolutely necessary to be there? How many times did you run in just for a jug of milk or a loaf of bread and you came out with a shopping cart full of stuff? Light, bright, cheerful, scientifically arranged and stocked -- the atmosphere invites us to buy as much as we can -- and we do!

Too tired to go out after work, or you can't sleep? Turn on the TV. Flip around the channels and there it is -- The TV Shopping Bazaar going strong, 24 hours a day. You just happened to catch a glimpse of a dazzling 14k gold necklace being pitched by super salespersons Hank Hunk and gorgeous Gloria Glitz. Even if you don't really want the trinket, what a thrill if you get to talk on national TV with these polished performers who will stroke you to death with their overbearing gushiness! "Well, hi," coos Ms. Glitz. "What's *your* name? (First names only, folks. We don't really want to know who you are!) Well, Lester, con-grat-u-lations! Whoooo! Aren't you lucky that you were able to get in on this deal! They're *really* going out the door! You've got yourself a fab-u-lous 14k gold necklace. Is it for yourself or your wife? Well, aren't you sweet to buy it for your grandma! Now, tell me Lester, how much do you think this would go for in your area? Remember, Lester, it's exquisitely hand-crafted Italian 14k gold, imported from Sicily, the cultural center of the world." Lester, who is neither a jeweler nor a smart jewelry shopper, and who thinks the world's cultural center is at the Hayseed Saloon on Saturday night, guesses it might go for a couple of hundred more and agrees he's got himself a real deal. Having jollied Lester into that instant appraisal, he's served his purpose. Ms. Glitz quickly ends the game: "Now you and your grandma, -- what's your grandma's name -- Thelma? -- you and Thelma enjoy, okay? Give her a hug for me and you take care, hear?" Click. Lester will be paying for that brief encounter with Ms. Glitz for the next 12 months. Of course, if his grandma doesn't like the necklace he can always send it back. But you know and they know Lester is not going to do that because it's too much trouble and besides, he bought it on the "we gotcha" easy payment plan.

Once again, let's affirm that you deserve to have gold chains and other things that give pleasure. But there are more important things you deserve too, and you won't have them if you fritter away your hard earned money on stuff you may soon forget you charged. How often have you opened your monthly charge card statement and asked yourself "When did I buy *that*?" Or "What *did* I buy from the TV Shopping Show?"

But the real pickpocket in your life is probably "The Mall" -- that Taj Mahal of architectural splendor that caters to and promotes reckless consumer spending. To seekers of instant gratification, the mall is irresitable. "I get total fulfillment from it," one woman said. "Shopping is like a drug," a man said. "It's a temporary high." ("Shopping Just For The Fun Of It," United Press Syndicate, January 17, 1988)

Malls are like banks, only more convenient because spenders can engage in "direct deposit." They cash their paychecks (perhaps at a bank branch in the mall) and directly desposit the cash in the stores in the mall. Instead of the interest that might be earned in a "real" bank, they get instant gratification. They immediately get unneeded or worthless "things" in exchange for the "direct deposit."

Malls are included in the general plan of a city as part of the controlled economy of a region. Although they provide jobs and services and contribute to the community's economic well being, that's not their primary function. *Malls are there to earn a return on an investment,* with money to build them provided by domestic and foreign entrepreneurs. As a matter of fact, many "American" businesses are now owned or controlled by wealthy foreign investors.

Master planned shopping centers are a far cry from the days before restrictive land use planning when an aspiring businessman could open a shop just about any place he felt he could prosper, which was usually on Main Street. More than likely he lived with his family in a "flat" over the business (just think -- he didn't have to fight freeway traffic and he didn't contribute to air pollution). His goal was to make a living for himself and his family by selling needed products or a service. He started on a shoestring with his own money. He didn't have or need an elaborate business plan that detailed how much profit he *had* to make by a certain date in order to pay back a staggering "start-up" loan arranged by a bank or investors.

The creation of malls has made possible a new type of venture: investment vehicles masquerading as *needed* businesses. You don't need what they sell but they need and want *your* money. Look at the number of "junk" eateries in the mall. Do you really need that purple popcorn, or the 12-inch chocolate chip cookie, or the corndog on a stick? Or that over-priced slice of pizza? No, you don't need any of it, but because it's there and it looks or smells good and you're kind of hungry, you buy it. Or how about the amusement arcade where you can drop a $10 roll of quarters in nothing flat. They're counting on us spending a lot and often, and so far, we haven't disappointed them!

When a business is opened and a pre-determined rate of return must be realized within a specific time, it means taking whatever action is necessary to get the public to buy, and *right now*. There can be no waiting until buyers get around to discovering the business exists. But not to worry! The behavioral scientists have us figured out to a "T". Using sophisticated market research and scientifically prepared advertising strategies, really "on the ball" business investors know before we do not only *what* we'll spend our money on, but *how much* we'll spend. They know well in advance that not only will we buy enough to pay the rent and expenses of doing business, but enough to provide a handsome profit for the investors who own the enterprise.

THE RICH GET RICHER WITH YOUR MONEY

What other gadgets, gizzmos and other "gotta have" stuff do you buy in the mall that you don't really need, and might not even want if you took time to think about it?

While there are literally thousands of examples of "things" people waste money on that could easily and profitably be done without, let's talk about all those records you buy. The record industry takes a tremendous bite out of *many* paychecks. Take for example, the "investment" you have made in rock star Peter Pervert. Never mind that the racket he makes and which we've been conditioned to accept as "music" is vulgar, and never mind that the lyrics to his "songs" promote everything from incest to suicide. Thanks to his adoring fans he's living very well, thank you. At the very minimum he has a multi-million dollar beach house at Malibu, perhaps a couple of doors down from Johnny Carson's place. He has a Porsche, a Rolls, and a Mercedes or two stashed at his Beverly Hills Estate. He can afford a stable of accountants and tax experts who will keep him living in luxury for the next 50 years, assuming of course, that his cocaine habit doesn't kill him before his next birthday. In the meantime, many of his fans who give up food or some other necessity to buy his albums or attend his "concerts" are living from paycheck to paycheck. Their prospects for a financially secure future are remote. Perhaps if he really cared about those who are sacrificing their earnings to provide him with a luxurious lifestyle now and in the future, -- perhaps if he really had some of the social conscience his public relations people say he has (okay, he *did* donate the proceeds of a "concert" to support the starving revolutionaries in Slobbovia), he'd offer to help his fans, right here in the good old U.S.A. learn how they can acquire a piece of the same good life he's enjoying. *Fat Chance.* The closest the fans will get to anything that even remotely resembles Mr. Pervert's "good life" is when it's showcased on TV's "Lifestyles of the Rich and Famous."

Moving right along with another example of mindless spending -- Do you *really* think you will be sexier, more desirable or "more" whatever if you buy (meaning, on your credit card, and for which you will pay 21 percent interest over the next 12 months) TV soap star Victoria Vixen's $120 an ounce "parfum," its scent oddly reminiscent of decaying fish? Do you *really* think she needs any more money, particularly *your* money? Sure she has a right to sell it and we wish her well -- but let those who can really afford it -- those who won't miss the $120 they got as a stock dividend -- let them buy it.

How much do you spend for exorbitantly priced potions that promise to stop or turn back time? Cosmetics that can't give you a thing except hope -- hope that if you spend $60 an ounce for skin cream you'll keep forever or acquire (depending on your age!) the same tight, flawless skin as the 20-year old beauty in the TV or magazine advertisements. The truth is we can smear anything from goose grease to mayonnaise to snake oil on our faces and bodies and while all the sticky stuff will alleviate dryness, temporarily giving a more youthful appearance, nothing will stop skin from aging. If we have good genes and take care of our health we'll look good longer. In the long run we'll be better off if we save our money and at the appropriate time hire a reputable cosmetic surgeon to repair the damage. That we can be snookered into believing we can turn back or hold off the ravages of time with a jar of *anything* is a tribute to the ability of the advertising industry to lie to us without really lying and to make a fortune for cosmetic companies in the bargain.

About clothing: Do you really need the costly

creations bearing the logo and label of the wealthy heiress, entertainer, or ex-princess turned "designer?" She needs *your* money about as much as your dog needs more fleas. Will wearing *her* creations with *her* name plastered across *your* chest or *your* fanny make you any more special or important than you already are? *Ah, but you buy her stuff because you like the quality.* Ah, but are you sure that's the reason? Do her expensive T-shirts shrink any less than a no-name T-shirt? If you are really impressed with the quality and that's *really* why you buy her wares, then take this test: Cut off the labels (if you can get them off without damaging the goods -- they are an important part of the merchandise and are meant to stay put) and ship them back to her with a letter explaining how much you like her designs but you don't like them well enough to work for her for nothing. Huh? What does *that* mean? It means that you now understand that Ms. Designer is using you and you are not going to be a noodnick anymore. See, you do *her* a favor when you buy her "designer" sweatsuit or whatever with her name and/or distinctive logo firmly attached in a location that can't be missed by everyone who sees you, from the front or rear. Ms. Designer, gutsy money maker that she is, in effect is saying, "Even though you plunked down your cash or put yourself into debt with your credit card for the privilege of wearing my over-priced fashions, I'm still not satisfied that I've gotten as much out of you as I can. Therefore, in return for allowing you to strut around with *my* la-de-da name that just reeks of riches on *your* very common body, you are going to work for me *free*, as a walking billboard each and every time you wear my clothes."

In a more genteel, less money grubbing era, clothing labels were discreetly hidden *inside* of clothes, at the neck, or on an inside pocket of a suit jacket. That you could afford to buy a "Princess Tacky" creation or "For Jocks Only" jeans was *your* secret. The quality or style of the garment spoke for itself and was a tribute to the wearer's good taste.

Obviously, it's not just clothing that is misused for advertising. Accessories such as watches, scarves, handbags, umbrellas and luggage, to name just a few, are just as bad. And don't forget the posters and household items such as cups, ashtrays and waste baskets bearing advertising for "Coke" or "Coors" or other brand names. Have these companies paid *you* to promote their products? If the answer is "no" then why should you *pay* to have the item? In less greedy times, businesses *gave away* items bearing the company name, and the company was most grateful for the opportunity to get the free advertising. Or, better yet, they were so thrilled to get your business they gave you gifts such as glasses or knives that were devoid of any advertising. *Weren't those the good old days!*

Think about it. If you've ever purchased advertising,

such as newspaper or magazine ads, TV or radio time, then you know it can be *very expensive*. Which means that if businesses had to pay consumers today's going rate for "advertising" a designer's clothes or displaying articles with their names on them, it would cost *big* bucks!

Good grief. Talk about being used!

Okay, here comes the obvious come-back: *We all drive cars with "brand names" on them. What do you have to say about that?* Just this: There isn't a choice. You can't buy a car without some kind of distinctive name or decoration on it. It's a take it or leave it situation. But you *do* have a choice when it comes to clothing or household items. You don't have to work without compensation to advertise clothing companies or those who manufacture or distribute the personal or household items you buy. *You have a choice.*

These businesspeople take advantage of our human frailty. They know the typical consumers who buy their merchandise will happily allow themselves to be used in exchange for the privilege of experiencing a vicarious status and feeling of importance that supposedly "rubs off" from wearing or having famous name items.

There are so *many* examples of "opportunities" to throw away your money that could be discussed, but surely you get the message. And certainly, you've thought about it yourself, many times. And undoubtedly, there have been times when you've been angry with yourself for falling prey to the slick money grabbers. But what to do? If you are unhappy with your shopping habits learn to ask yourself three questions before you take money or a credit card out of your pocket: Do I want it? (Silly question!) Do I need it? (Of course!) But here's the clincher: Can I do without it? If you are honest with yourself you'll find that you can answer "yes" to the last question more times than you might imagine. Try it. You'll be amazed how quickly your financial situation will improve.

You will also be impressed by the amount of money you save if you can resist "bargains" or "sales." If you really need a sale item and you *know* without a doubt it's a great buy -- it's something you really need or will enjoy -- then go for it. Otherwise, resist the temptation. Ask yourself -- if you buy the bargain that is supposed to save you money -- *what* will you save? Will you have the money you "saved" in your pocket?

Once again, please understand that no one is asking you to deprive yourself of having nice things. Life is too short not to enjoy it. Just keep in mind that it's *your money* that's the target and no one deserves to have it more than you do! Also keep in mind that it's not *your* personal responsibility to keep the economy afloat by spending everything you earn. *Let somebody else take that "reponsibility" more often.*

Think about it.

It could (and should) be argued that wealthy

practitioners and supporters of free enterprise and capitalism have a right to set up shop and prosper. After all, this is America. We just need to develop an awareness that shopping malls, supermarkets, TV shopping clubs and other "opportunities" to get rid of our money are "attractive nuisances" that we should use prudently, instead of allowing them to use us.

The advertising industry isn't going to tell you this, so consider it our secret: If shopping is therapeutic for you; if you simply must reach into your purse or pocket and pull out money and hand it over to a cashier in return for something you imagine you *must have now*, try shopping at your local Goodwill or other thrift store. It's amazing what you can find there. Not only do people give away some great pieces of clothing, but it's obvious that some of the items the Goodwill receives have never been used -- just overstock or "out of season" from clothing stores. After a trip to the dry cleaners or a spin through the clothes washer for sanitation's sake, who's going to know your new outfit isn't new?

If you are not interested in classy or new-looking clothes, but prefer the "ragged and ratty" skid-row look that is currently the *ultimate* fashion statement, why pay department store prices when you can get the same trashy look for a whole lot less at a thrift shop? And just think -- you'll be contributing to a good cause at the same time. If "distressed denim" is "hot" -- just take some thrift-shop jeans or other articles of clothing and arrange an accident with a jug of chlorine bleach. You may discover creativity you never knew you had!

It's interesting that when you tell some people you buy clothing at a thrift shop they give you a funny look and may even recoil from your presence. At social gatherings they'll gossip about it. If they say anything to your face it usually goes like this: "Yuck! Buy clothes at a thrift shop? Have you ever seen the people who go there?" Well, how would they know unless they've been there too??? The fact is, *all kinds* of people frequent thrift shops. Probably among them are well-to-do ladies who like to save money and as a result of their thrifty habits live in a nicer neighborhood than most of us! But look, those folks who disdain thrift shopping are not really snobs. They just care about your health. For example, they will also say, "Aren't you afraid of catching *something*?" My response is that just by living you take a chance of catching *something*. The point is, those thrift-shoppers who may be lice-infested or worse, also try on clothes in ritzy department stores, or haven't you noticed? How do you know who has tried on the jeans you just tried on?

Again, and again and again: Nobody deserves to have your money more than you do! Don't ever forget it.

It is a tragic and ugly truth that goes unrecognized

and unspoken: *The American worker is little more than a dehumanized mechanical pump that is constantly primed to keep money in circulation. John and Jane Worker are the ultimate perpetual motion bread machines that grind out the dough for others to feast upon.* Think about it: isn't that the way it really is? Is it disgusting? You bet it is.

The good news is that it doesn't have to be that way. You have a tremendous amount of power over what happens to your money. *You can fight the system and win.* The very next paycheck you receive, look at it thoughtfully before you deposit it in your checking account or cash it. Tell yourself over and over again, "It's mine. Beyond my absolutely necessary fixed expenses no one has a right to it except me. I earned it. I'll spend it when I please and how I please and *if* I please." Learn to respect what it represents -- all the hours out of your life, all of the effort, all of the sweat, maybe even the tears -- that it took to get it. Once you acknowledge and assert your right to control what's yours, you'll see how quickly you can get ahead financially, -- in spite of a poor education; in spite of manipulative advertising; in spite of peer pressure; in spite of *anything.*

Now, let's explore what you have to go through and put up with to get the money that you keep in circulation so efficiently and reliably.

Our relationship with our "work family" is not a democratic affair. By whatever name, plain or fancy, a boss is still a boss, whose bidding we do, like it or not because "it's our job" and we go along to get along. Which is okay.

But what is so damn irritating is that while we are supposed to behave and think of ourselves as "family" on the job, in most cases, that loyalty is not repaid in kind by our employer.

It's such a lop-sided relationship: WE go the extra mile; WE bend over backwards to prove our worth; WE put in overtime when we know there will be no monetary compensation; WE are grateful to have the lousy job.

If we retire without a pension, or other tangible, worthwhile benefits, we are strictly on our own. With just the memories and the realization that we were such fools to give our all in return for so little, including having to cope with the brutal, daily pain of not being able to make ends meet.

Old age is not a TV mini-series that is over in five nights. It is the ultimate long-term contract that expires when we do. And it's certainly not prime-time unless we have prepared extremely well for it.

3

The Price You Pay For A Job

Our economic system, which is no longer true "free enterprise," but rather, something closer to monopolistic capitalism, is still the best system in the world in terms of providing the means to attain a high standard of living for those who are willing to work.

With all its faults, real or imagined; in spite of how badly true free enterprise has been hobbled by adverse social, political, judicial and government intervention -- in spite of everything -- there is nothing to compare with it. In general, the lifestyle enjoyed by most Americans and envied by much of the world is evidence that our system works. Therefore, discussion in the previous chapter of the excesses of advertising and the impact of "spending opportunities" should not be misunderstood as an attack on any business or the American way of "doing business." We just need to learn to use the system to *our* advantage which, unfortunately, is easier said than done.

NEW TYRANNY
IN THE WORKPLACE

Even though our economic system permits a high stardard of living, it does have a "down" side. The very freedom that allows the system to work also allows employers to engage in all kinds of behavior which becomes a two-edged sword for workers. On the one hand it gives business owners, upper level decision makers and managers the opportunity to exercise decency and compassion in dealing with workers. On the other hand, that same freedom allows abuse and exploitation of those who are hired to produce profit.

But didn't abuse and exploitation cease with elimination of sweat shops, enactment of child labor laws, establishment of unions and all the other benefits that supposedly resulted from the turmoil of the industrial revolution? True, gone is the hot, dirty sweatshop in which children and women toiled long hours for obscenely indecent wages. Gone is the ogre of a boss who had not one shred of human compassion. *Hallelujah! It's over!*

Sorry, it's not over. It's just taken a new form.

There is a new Orwellian version of the pre-industrial revolution workplace inhumanity and it's called Management by Objectives, generally referred to as MBO. It is also known as Planning Programming Budgeting System (PPBS) and other less familiar names.

MBO is an ultra efficient system of business and people management. The cold, flashy glass and steel office buildings in which MBO thrives give a clue to the "nature of the beast." They have a "charisma" that projects a feeling of power. Their interiors are environmentally perfect, impeccably furnished and decorated to promote maximum productivity and at the same time, job satisfaction. Scientifically selected background music, played at just the right sound level, may be imbedded with subliminal messages urging honesty or promoting greater productivity. There generally isn't a great deal of "hustle and bustle." There is an "aura" that suggests *everything is under control*.

And it is. Control is what MBO is all about.

Many, if not most businesses, particularly large, multinational businesses, are operated by this system. In a company that utilizes MBO, the worker becomes an inanimate replaceable tool -- a "thing" that is used to achieve specific goals and objectives. A detailed lock-step job description is written for the task to be performed by the tool (the worker). Each step or activity is specific to insure that the job behavior will contribute to reaching the designated goals. Computers keep everything and everyone in line and on target.

Managers and supervisors are held accountable for reaching the goals. Therefore, they must do whatever it takes, and will treat workers in whatever manner is necessary to produce work that will achieve the goals. Bosses have been trained to use sophisticated behavior modification techniques to manipulate workers without their even suspecting they've been robbed of their humanity.

If the company is really intent on getting the most productivity out of rank and file employees, it may invest in scientifically developed programs designed to alter attitudes and values. Unfortunately, there can be some pretty devastating "fallout" after a worker is run through one of these "wringers." It has been documented many times that the resultant behavior change may be so drastic that it causes family problems. For example, the spouse and/or children may not be able to cope with the newly acquired aggressive behavior of the "new" person living with them.

As an alternative to such programs, maximum productivity may be squeezed out of employees by a slick motivational speaker. The result is not as drastic and will make a marked improvement in employee output for a reasonable period of time.

After the "treatment" is over employees may be timed to see how long it takes to perform a task. Or they may be observed through one-way glass.

Sure, the larger-than-life mean and ugly boss is gone from view. Now he watches from afar, using a stopwatch, a high-tech peephole and a computer to chart and analyze productivity. *It's called progress.*

Since managerial and supervisory personnel are held accountable for results, they, too, are subject to performance review and corrective behavior modification. But while a worker is given corrective "treatment" on the job, upper level management people may be sent away for a weekend "retreat" where they are worked over with the latest psychological mind games and gimmicks designed to improve their performance.

Doesn't all that sound like fun? Only if your mind is warped. And it tends to get that way after enough "experts" have been digging around inside your head and yanking at your emotions with manipulative activities.

Yes, it is Orwellian and idiots that we are, we continue to delude ourselves with the fantasy that we are free agents; that what we have become is of our own choosing.

It bears repeating: There is no "humanity" inherent in the Management by Objectives system of business operation. It is totally oriented toward ever-increasing levels of profit, productivity and growth. Which of itself, is not evil. When companies don't grow and prosper, they stagnate and die. The point is, *MBO does not recognize you as a human being.* MBO does not use *people* to reach goals, it uses *tools.* That the tools happen to be human beings is of no importance. *Tools are tools.*

THE PRICE OF EFFICIENCY: "JOB RELATED STRESS"

A by-product of the Management by Objectives system has been labeled "job related stress" which is manifested in an assortment of emotional and physical symptoms. Certainly there always has been stress in the workplace, but in times past the causes were more obvious -- the blatantly abusive boss, or the inhumane working conditions. Today, causes of stress are often less identifiable. The MBO system that is responsible for (or at least, significantly contributes to) the stress is rarely implicated as a possible culprit. Few people seem able (or are willing?) to target *exactly* what's wrong. So instead of dealing with reality and attempting to identify root causes when "people problems" arise, the company hires specialists to teach employees to use stress reduction techniques such as group therapy, "therapeutic touch," meditation, guided imagery, visualization or self-hypnosis. Many workers object to these approaches to behavior change because they are in conflict with ethical or religious beliefs. But that's of no concern to the company. *Like it or lump it. Take it or leave it. Achievement of corporate goals comes first. The system doesn't change to accommodate the human needs or concerns of workers -- the workers are manipulated to adjust to the system.*

Even in the absence of ethical objections, by sheer instinct most workers know that mind bending is not right but they "go with the flow." After all, their paycheck arrives on a regular schedule, doesn't it?

So, to get back to the original question: Didn't abuse and exploitation cease with elimination of sweat shops, enactment of child labor laws, establishment of unions and all the other benefits that supposedly resulted from the turmoil of the industrial revolution? The answer has to be: *Only appearances have changed.* The physical and environmental abuses of a bygone era have been replaced by insidious mental and emotional stresses, which are even more abusive because too often they aren't clearly recognized for what they are. If you think about it, "job related stress" has been recognized as a problem only fairly recently -- since MBO has become widespread, not only in business, but in education and at all levels of government.

The reality is that George Orwell's vision of 1984 in which workers are controlled and treated as if they are mindless robots has come to pass -- give or take a couple of years. But because we are still allowed to have ample food and pleasure, most people haven't noticed they are now shackled in invisible chains.

THIS IS THE WAY LIFE IS FOR MOST OF US. . .

We've gotten ahead of things. Let's start at the beginning of your work life. You graduate from or drop out of high school or college and get a job. Five days a week, maybe six, 50 or more weeks a year, for 40 or more years, you get up and go to work. *Until you retire or die, your life is controlled by your work.*

People have a broad range of feelings about the work experience. Many are very happy with what they do for a living. They have a dream job that is emotionally and financially rewarding. They are doing just what they want to do and they are right where they want to be. These lucky people are not the majority, however.

In between are those who tell you their job is okay. Just *okay*. There isn't a lot of growth potential, but that's *okay*. The pay is adequate and there isn't a whole lot of stress. They know what's expected and they do the best they can. It's a tolerable place to spend the best hours and days of your life. What helps make the job *okay* are the "little things" -- nice co-workers, pleasant surroundings, and adequate recognition. Being designated "employee of the month" or receiving a flowery note from the boss goes a long way in contributing to job satisfaction for many people. To keep employees on their best behavior, some companies hire "shoppers" who reward zealous employees with a "gold star" like you used to get in kindergarden for not wetting your pants. Most workers happily accept these "warm 'n fuzzy strokes" without thinking about what an insult they really are to an industrious adult. Wouldn't something extra in the pay envelope be more appropriate? Wouldn't it show that the company *really* valued your work enough to make an award that would help pay the bills?

The okay job becomes a rotten job for the employee who wants to achieve a certain income level but because he is lacking what it takes to get ahead (better or more education, specialized training) there is a lot of frustration and even rage that may be expressed in destructive, anti-social behavior such as theft or drug abuse. He wonders: should he move on and in essence, start over again in a new job that may be more promising? He can't afford to take time off to go back to school so he stays where he is and hopes the Job Fairy will happen along and hand him the opportunity he's been dreaming of.

A little bit farther down the line are those who

have dreams and goals -- the young and very restless. Let's say it's *you*. You may spend your days in a huge windowless office, surrounded by an army of people who are doing the same boring work you are doing. Most of them are hankering for advancement but each sees the other as a stumbling block to a promotion. You have to put up with office politics, insidious and divisive gossip, varying kinds and degrees of harassment and intrigues, not to mention the accompanying stress.

To the company you are a faceless clone, differentiated only by an employee number. You are a necessary evil whose sole purpose is to contribute to corporate profit and growth. If the corporation could get along without you, it would do so. Right now they may be thinking about how to replace you with a computer. After all, you're just a replaceable tool -- a thing. You tough it out because there does seem to be a light at the end of the tunnel. Others have moved up the corporate ladder. Maybe you can too.

At the far end of the spectrum are employees with a love-hate relationship with their job. Perhaps this is your situation? You love it because it pays great and there is nothing else you could do that would pay more. You hate it because working conditions are lousy, to put it politely. Your biggest gripe is that you are worked to death in exchange for the better than average salary. There isn't enough help to handle the workload so one employee must do the work of two.

If it takes overtime to get the work done, you are expected to give the extra effort and time cheerfully, and unless you have a union contract that spells things out in detail and it is set in concrete, chances are you may not be paid for the extra effort. After all, you're doing it *for the company*. And beside that, aren't they paying you more than you deserve, anyway? So you put up and shut up because you have to eat and pay your bills.

Your working environment may be smoky, drafty, too hot, too cold, smelly, dirty and generally not conducive to feeling and doing your best. Perhaps a chair isn't provided because sitting down is frowned upon. Which probably doesn't matter anyway since you must be constantly on the go. You may not have time on some days to eat your brown bag lunch or take a potty break. And speaking of necessities, the restrooms might not have been cleaned in six months because Sara, the nice clerk-typist, decided one day that it wasn't going to be her responsibility anymore. It's not that the company can't afford a maintenance service -- business is good -- but cheapskate that it is, it just doesn't want to spend the money. The corporate thinking is that when someone with delicate sensibilities finally gets sick of looking at the cruddy sink and toilet, eventually that same someone will break down and clean it up.

Regardless of what you do, or how much you like

or dislike your job, there is one thing common to all jobs, even those "dream" jobs: You are supposed to be constantly thinking about how to promote the business, how to bring in more customers, how to increase sales, how to boost profits. In other words, you are supposed to pretend the business is yours, when in fact, you have no financial interest in it, other than performing an honest day's work for a day's pay.

If you are working for a growing company it may be argued that as the company grows and prospers, you will, too. Maybe so. But everybody knows someone who gave her all *for the company* -- worked many unpaid hours, swept floors, ran errands with her own car and the company did indeed grow and prosper, but in the end all the eager employee had to show for the dedication were stubs from paychecks and a bonus or two. The company didn't even have the decency to offer profit sharing after the business really took off. *Yes, the company is a demanding god.*

At this point let's understand that everyone should earn their keep. When we agree to do a job it should be done to the best of our ability whether or not we like the job. An employer has a right to expect that we will capably and conscientiously perform the work we were hired to do. Furthermore, it's the honorable thing to do and a job well done does wonders to boost self-esteem. And you never know when you'll need a good reference for another job. Your reputation *does* matter.

LIFE ON THE JOB: IS IT REAL OR A SOAP OPERA?

Having to put up with a less than perfect employer is one thing. If you must also contend with the public you may have an added set of problems. Between the two you can often find yourself on the brink of going totally bananas.

Anyone who has been dealing with the public for at least 25 years will agree that the attitude and behavior of consumers of all ages have changed. Today *many* people are impatient, dishonest, envious, anxious and just plain filled with rage. And why are they this way? The answer can be summed up in one word: *Money. There isn't enough money.* Not having enough money to obey all the messages to buy everything under the sun is compounded by peer pressure to use alcohol, cocaine, pot or other drugs that can burn up a week's pay (and a whole lot more!) in nothing flat. The incessant prodding to spend comes smack up against the reality of limited income. If that isn't enough to make you crazy, then what is?

Not having enough money makes even basically honest people ready to milk the most out of every situation. Whipped into an "I ain't gonna be cheated" frenzy by consumer advocates, some of whom have a questionable political agenda, the public has become very much aware of its "rights." Certainly, the public *does* have rights and today more than ever we need to be aware of increasing numbers of unscrupulous shysters masquerading as legitimate businesses. But sometimes the perception of what is a "right" is misunderstood.

For example, here is just one incident in the day of a pharmacist that is a good example of "to hell with you I got my rights and I come first and I want it now" consumerism. Multiply it by a dozen times a day, five days a week. After reading the following account you will probably say, "that's nothing -- you should see what I have to put up with" -- and no one would doubt you for one moment. Anyway, consider this:

It's 8:45 a.m. and the pharmacy department of the store where you are employed to help heal the sick and comfort the hurting is not yet open but there are six people waiting, each clutching one or more prescriptions. They see you coming and start to close in. Before you can get behind the counter and without so much as a "good morning" one of them shoves a prescription in your hand. "How long do I have to wait, I've got to get to work," he barks. Almost simultaneously another butts in with "Why do you open so late? All the while the phone has been ringing nonstop. You have no help so you are all things to all people. Even though it's clear that God gave you only one head and two hands, everybody is unhappy that they have to wait. As you crank up the computer and go through necessary opening routines, an irate senior citizen bangs his cane on the counter and hollers at you, "Why are you taking so long?" Never mind that yesterday this Dear Old Frog, who thinks that having lived 80 years gives him a license to be abusive, had a 2 o'clock appointment with the doctor who didn't get to see him until three hours later -- *he wants his prescriptions filled now!*

But are you ready for this? In the middle of all the commotion, maneuvering her way to the head of the line that has formed is none other than Heidi Hotsheetz, a Donna Mills look-alike. She's hanging on the arm of her Sylvester Stallone clone whose demeanor clearly states, "Serve us first or there's going to be trouble." Pretending no one else is there she girlishly bounces up and down a couple of times and trills sweetly, "Hi e e e! I'm Heidi Hotsheetz and I'm here to pick up my prescription for my birth control pills." You intuitively sense this sweet little cookie is trouble with a capital "T" and you just want to get rid of her as quickly as possible even if it means letting others wait a little longer.

While you go to get her prescription she seizes the moment and gives her boyfriend a smooch. Alas, all you can find is a note from the previous pharmacist on duty saying that Heidi used all her refills and must have the doctor's permission for another. You go back out to the counter and give her the bad news. Faster than it takes to blink an eye she turns hostile and informs you in no uncertain terms that she does have another refill on that prescription. Such convincing acting you have yet to see on The Young and the Restless. To placate her you go back to the computer and double check. It's clear that a mistake has *not* been made.

Meanwhile the people who were waiting before Ms. Hotsheetz barged in are beginning to show signs of combativeness, and who could blame them? They are pacing back and forth, shooting dirty looks your way and mumbling to each other about the horrible service. On top of it, another half dozen people have arrived including: A mother carrying a crying baby with an earache; a woman needing medication to control the pain of a wisdom tooth extraction; a senior citizen leaning on a walker who wants her arthritis medicine. The phone is still ringing off the hook and because you can't do two things at the same time, you ignore it. But someone else in the store answers it and calls over the intercom "pharmacist pick up on line two".

During the momentary pause caused by the announcement, an unclean person thrusts a contagious looking arm in front of your face and demands an instant diagnosis: "Hey, what's good for this rash?" Annoyed by the interruption, Ms. Hotsheetz has set her jaw defiantly, and menacingly placed her hands on her hips. In other words, she ain't leavin' until she gets what she came for. She wants those birth control pills, and she wants them *now.*

Feeling battle-weary even before the day has begun, you make a snap decision. Time to stop being Ms. Niceperson. You look her straight in her cold baby blue eyes and tell her you have no intention of jeopardizing your license to practice pharmacy by dispensing unauthorized medication. She is simply going to have to wait until her doctor gives permission. End of discussion. It's really sad. You feel like patting this misguided volcano of raging hormones on the head and telling her something she may not have heard before, even from her mother: "Hey, it's okay not to have sex for 24 hours! You'll survive!"

To make things worse, Ms. Hotsheetz will probably report you to management and you will be counseled on how to properly treat customers. But you see, management hasn't had the pleasure of having to deal with the likes of a Heidi Hotsheetz, at least not recently, holed up as they are in the protective cocoon of the corporate ivory tower. You know where that is, don't you? It's up on the lushly carpeted sixteenth floor awash in calming colors and soothing music.

And management isn't faced with customers who engage in scary behavior. For example, an irate, irrational, spaced-out "customer" recently called my husband a "sh*%@#y old man" and threatened his life because he refused to sell him insulin syringes. The customer couldn't tell him what kind of insulin was to be used in the syringes. My husband has a rigid rule: if you don't know what kind of insulin you need, you don't need syringes. Period. But it's risky if you choose not to aid and abet drug abuse. When the druggies need a fix, absolutely nothing else matters.

These days there is a great deal of "abuse awareness." Awareness of child abuse; spouse abuse; parent abuse; elder abuse; animal abuse; environment abuse. And it's about time that we as a supposedly civilized society came to grips with the horror of these abuses, particularly those that affect the physical and emotional health and safety of human beings. But how often do you hear about "job abuse" -- the hurt inflicted by greedy, uncaring employers or demanding, insensitive customers?

The point of airing the above examples of less than ideal working conditions is to bring into focus the reality that *everyone* who works, particularly with the public, has to put up with a lot of stress and disrespect. There is no "Job Abuse Anonymous" support group or Ralph Nader-type advocates to go to bat for the "job abused." For the most part you simply have to grin and bear it, because *it's your job.*

Certainly, there are a lot of nice, considerate, patient people that you meet on your job every day and you thank God for every last one of this vanishing breed. But without a doubt, what used to be called "common decency" appears to be going the way of the dinosaur.

And to be perfectly fair, there are times when obnoxious customer behavior is a result of company policies. For example, if the company is too cheap to provide enough help so that customers can be helped in a manner in which they should be helped, they may have good cause to be grouchy. When a company expects an employee to do the work of two or more workers, it's difficult, not only to do the job, but to do it with a positive attitude about either the customer or the company. After all, the employee is just as human as the customer and is just as much a product of the times. Why should the employee be expected to exhibit super-human qualities?

What a pity some companies don't understand that if loyalty and maximum productivity are expected from employees, optimum working conditions *must* be provided. You could deal with the likes of Heidi Hotsheetz and all the rest of the difficult people if only you had the support to do it. The benefit would show up as *profit. Lots of it.* Isn't that what Corporate America wants? *Sometimes, you wonder.*

AFTER IT'S ALL OVER

When it's all over and you've reached retirement, shouldn't you have more to show for your time and best efforts beside emotional scars, an abused and battered psyche, an ulcer, paycheck stubs, a stingy retirement plan and paltry Social Security checks? Except for the brief time you spent on the way to work or on the way home you didn't hear the birds, smell the flowers or see the sunshine and blue sky. If you have children, while you and your spouse worked they were raised by baby sitters, teachers, TV and peers. When they became teenagers you tore out your hair because you suddenly realized that their values were not *your* values but a composite of the values of all the strangers who had more access to them than you did.

It's incredible when you think about it. Most of the best hours and days or your life are not yours. You trade them for paychecks. Is it a fair trade for *you*?

Clearly, something is terribly out of balance. Our way of doing business, as great as it is could be even greater if Corporate America would abandon its adversarial attitude toward workers. After all, workers and employers are "in it together" -- like it or not.

It's time to rethink the worker-employer relationship. It's time to treat employees as the valuable part of the team they really are and to recognize that they sacrifice the best years of their lives "for the company."

It's time to shift the focus from "we're the master, you're the servant" to "let us do the best we can for each other."

American businesses are notoriously generous to good causes, although the giving may be motivated by good publicity or tax considerations. Which is perfectly alright. When you have money you can spend it however you like, and so much the better if it serves several good purposes at the same time.

But corporate philanthropy is hypocritical in the absence of long-term benefits for employees (all employees, not just top management) such as a substantial pension, meaningful profit sharing, or at least, financial planning assistance. More bluntly, it's pretty crummy.

It's crummy because the labor of those employees produced the profit that allows the giving. Even if a company can't afford a pension plan, or profit sharing, it can afford compassion and concern. It can offer to help employees successfully build their own financial security. It can adopt the attitude that "because we ask a lot of you as a worker, we care a lot about you as a human being. We will help you, the lifeblood of our business, before we help those who are not part of our corporate family."

Amen, brothers and sisters?

4

What Corporate America Can And Should Do

The company that employs you calls the shots. It has what you need to live and get along -- a job and the paycheck. In return for that job and paycheck you are supposed to be grateful -- and that's okay -- you should be, particularly if you are satisfied with the job, working conditions and pay. But look at it this way too: If you are a good employee, and most employees *are* good employees; if you go the "extra mile" even when it isn't required; if you are loyal, honest and dependable -- *you are a valuable asset to the company*. They should feel lucky to have you. So lucky, in fact, that they are willing to treat you as they would treat a financial partner or investor -- as someone *special*. Meaning, they should be willing to go the extra mile for *you.*

Any investor expects and receives a return on his money and he should. While you are not a partner in the sense that you have invested money, you *are* investing your time, effort and abilities. As a worker who does his best, you, too, deserve and should expect a return on *your* investment in a form other than your paycheck, transitory perks, or a even a pension.

Traditional corporate thinking is that nobody is indispensable (that's true!) and those employees who are not satisfied with any aspect of their job can look for employment elsewhere. So why should the company give anything more than it absolutely has to when replacements are relatively easy to find?

Even though there are more workers than there are corporations, the reality is that Corporate America couldn't exist without workers. Think about it. If your company couldn't get good, reliable workers where would it be?

Okay, where would workers be if the company didn't exist? Clearly, both employer and employee are absolutely necessary. If it takes Employer plus Employees to equal Maximum Production and Profit, shouldn't employees benefit accordingly?

As workers we need to see ourselves and our relationship with our employer in a new light. For too long we've accepted our status uncritically, accepting "crappy" treatment and generally taking what's dished out to us without complaint because "that's the way it's always been done" or "that's the way the system works." Where is it written in concrete that any and all kinds of attitudes and behavior must be accepted as the price that is paid for a job?

ALWAYS LOOKING OUT FOR NUMBER ONE

Corporate America is not crazy about making changes that benefit employees, even when insignificant amounts of money are involved. But when it comes to providing services that benefit the company, action can be swift. For example, to attract or keep capable workers an in-house day care center may be set up. To increase employee productivity exercise equipment may be installed. To stop problems caused by drugs or alcohol, a counseling center may be established. Poor job performance caused by poor reading ability is forcing many companies to provide remedial reading programs.

Yes, Corporate America can do and does whatever it makes up its corporate mind to do!

Every financially successful company has written goals and objectives relating to achievement of predermined levels of profit, productivity and growth. There is absolutely no reason or excuse for not having written goals relating to long-range financial benefits for workers.

Specifically, Corporate America must assist employees -- all employees -- right down to the men and women who mop the floors -- to be financially secure at retirement, or even before.

Do we hear howls of protest? "That's not the responsibility of the company." If we're going to be picky, neither is daycare, and neither are remedial reading programs, and neither is drug abuse counseling. But Corporate America *does* provide these services because it's "good business."

A business *must* care about the financial future of employees and how they will live and survive after they've given the best years of their lives to the company. The company *must* be willing and eager to provide the education, motivation and on-going direction that will enable employees to provide for their own future financial security.

It must be absolutely clear that when we say corporations must do more for employees we're not promoting handouts or advocating compulsion. The word *must* is used as a moral imperative. Nobody, no business in a free society should be *forced* to do more for employees than common decency and justice require. What employees agree to do that is legal and moral in exchange for a paycheck is up to them. What a corporation chooses to do *over and above* discharging its part of the bargain is up to the company. We are simply arguing for a new, progressive corporate conscience relating to employees -- the lifeblood of the business.

WORKING FOR PEANUTS PRODUCES CAVIAR PROFITS

Millions of Americans hold part-time or temporary jobs, not by choice but of necessity. Family responsibilities, health or age restrictions, or education plans make it impossible to work the usual 40-hour week.

In addition to less than optimal income the penalty paid for the flexibility of part-time work is high. Because of the "disposable diaper" status of part-timers they are generally paid less and receive few if any benefits. Understandably, hard-nosed profit oriented employers prefer these workers who are said to make up 25 percent of the American workforce.

Part-timers are found in all kinds of jobs but many of them work very hard in low paying service occupations, particularly in fast food restaurants. Traditionally, fast food jobs have been filled by energetic teenagers, eager to get their start in the adult world. However, a shortage of teens has forced fast food employers to recruit from all age groups with the focus on a growing supply of not-so-eager but short-of-cash retirees. Faced with inadequate retirement income and unanticipated expenses, many seniors are willing to work for minimum wage or slightly above it. Most of them are not working for fun or to stay busy. If they were just in search of a good time they'd be traveling in their RV, visiting grandchildren, touring Europe, playing golf, socializing at the community senior center or doing any number of pleasant things mature people like to do. When you ask a "fast food senior" how he or she likes the work the usual reply is, "It gets me out of the house and the people are nice." If questioned a bit more, a different picture begins to emerge. Admitted one senior, "Around 11 a.m. my ankles start to swell." When they are willing to put up with physical discomfort, you know for sure they are not working just for fun and companionship.

IMPERSONAL LONG DISTANCE LOVE

One fast food chain in particular is very community oriented and makes a great effort to project an image of having a strong social conscience. It sponsors a variety of events designed to raise money for cancer victims and other deserving causes, which is very commendable. A lot of people have been helped tremendously by such efforts. The chain's principal stockholder generously gives a significant amount of money to an assortment of charities which in turn results in priceless free publicity for the company. However, some of the political causes that are recipients of the largesse could be considered highly questionable. As just one example, $1 million in company stock has been donated to support a Soviet arts festival held in San Diego, California in 1990. Prior to leaving on an 18-day trip to the Soviet Union, the Mayor of San Diego said, "Going to the Soviet Union with $1 million in a bank account. . . will go a long way toward showing the Soviet Union that San Diego is committed to holding this festival." ("Joan Kroc Gives City $1 Million For 1990 Soviet Arts Festival," *San Diego Union*, June 22, 1988)

Shall we all throw up now, or later? *One million in stock for a Soviet arts festival?!* Okay, let's allow that an arts festival *may* help advance the cause of world peace. The emphasis is on *may* since the Soviets historically use cultural events to promote communism and there is no evidence to believe that anything has changed. As a matter of fact, Soviet leader Gorbachev has said, "We are not retreating even one step from socialism, from Marxism-Leninism, from everything that has been gained. . . " ("Gorbachev Calls for Progress on Political Reform," *Los Angeles Times*, February 19, 1988)

How many low-paid workers ran their legs off fetching fries and burgers and put up with customers who are often less than civil to these *always* cheerful employees, in order to produce the profit that allows such generous philanthropy? When workers can produce profit that allows megabucks to be given to charitable causes, but at the same time, there isn't a solid investment plan in place for those employees, isn't something out of balance? Even a tiny fraction of that $1 million spent on acquiring the services of a crack financial planner would go a long way toward helping those low-paid workers achieve financial independence. Doesn't the company realize that unless those employees are encouraged and helped to help themselves they will never have very much of anything? Doesn't the company care that the promise of "fun, friends and flexible hours" offered as a trade-off for low wages won't mean a *damn thing* when they want to buy a house or retire? *Charity should begin at home!*

Here's another typical example of "long distance love." Said a spokesman for an Eastern defense contractor, "We try to be very supportive of things that make a community a good place to live and work - music, dance and all the social services." ("Corporations Lend A Hand To The Needy," *Washington Post* May 16, 1988) While recognizing the noble intent of the company's generosity, it's tempting to say "stuff it in your hat," if the company hasn't first made certain that it has done as much as it can for its employees -- those whose labor makes possible contributions for "music, dance and all the social services."

Why is it so difficult to see that it's the decent and honorable thing to do -- to show concern for the welfare of "your own" before you throw money around for causes that may be questionable? Why is it so easy to practice "long distance love" -- to give to and do for those you can't see or don't know, and so difficult to care about those around you who are working so hard on your behalf? *Why the godawful stinginess with those who deserve generosity the most?*

But look, let's not get carried away. When you have money you can do with it as you darn well please, and nobody should tell you how to spend it. *Nevertheless*, as commendable as it is to give to needy strangers, *please*, take care of "family" *first*.

"THEY DON'T CARE" -- WHO SAYS?

It may be argued that young fast food and other low-paid service workers wouldn't have the interest or motivation to save and invest for their future, even if they were helped. Who says? What evidence is there to support such a claim since providing investment assistance hasn't been tried on a scale that would show it does or doesn't produce positive results? It may also be argued that it would never work because workers move around from job to job. *Perhaps workers might be inclined to stay put and show a greater interest in the business if the company showed a greater interest in them!* The cost of hiring and training a constant parade of "start and stop" workers can be considerable; an expense that quite possibly could be significantly reduced with just a little extra concern for employees.

And so what if they move from job to job? Why not get them started? If things were the way they should be, they could get the same kind of assistance at the next place of employment and pick up right where they left off. And think about this, too: Many low paid service workers are not between college semesters, working for spending money or just killing time until that "real job" opens up. They simply don't have the education or skills that will allow them to move up to higher paying jobs. They've found their niche in the work world. But they still have the same dreams and aspirations as everybody else. Let's face it: *Everybody* wants to be financially secure. No one enjoys doing without, depending on government handouts, or just scraping by with no prospect in sight for a brighter future. Look at the amount of money the poor and not so poor "invest" in lotteries, racetracks and gambling casinos in the hope of striking it rich.

It may take a lot of education and on-going encouragement and guidance, but again, so what?

Maybe such an attempt would fail but it doesn't have to. In any case, we won't know until we try, will we?

HOW IT COULD
BE FOR THE
NEXT GENERATION

All of the financial pain retirees are experiencing today, and which those right behind them will experience to an even greater degree, could have been avoided if early in their working years the giants of the business world had volunteered to be role models for a new standard of corporate responsibility. How different things might be today if even one major employer had issued and carried through with the following proclamation:

Because your efforts and dedication make possible our continuing growth and prosperity, and because the effect of your labor and loyalty today will be multiplied many times over for the benefit of the company long after you are gone, we want to help you grow and prosper, too. Therefore, during your productive years we are going to work hard to provide you with the best "here and now" benefits possible. In addition, we are going to try to make certain that at retirement you will be financially secure. We don't want you to be dependent on others, particularly the government. We want to make sure you are not, in effect, the blind man standing on a street corner with a tin cup begging strangers for money. You are the backbone of this company and of our nation and you deserve the best we can offer. After you've given us the best years of your life, helping you to live in dignity is the least we can do for you.

Therefore we would like to help you -- not give to you, but help you -- develop and put into action an on-going, long-term financial plan for your retirement. We would like to do this by helping you invest in our economic system. This is in addition to the company pension which may not be enough.

We would like to help you find and implement a plan with a demonstrated track record that employs sound investment principles. It will be a program that you can comfortably live with. There is absolutely no reason why only the "rich" or "lucky" or "shrewd" should take advantage of and profit from a system that offers spectacular opportunities to those who are willing to intelligently participate in it. Unions constantly exhort workers to "Buy American." That's good advice. It could be made better by adding, "And let's invest in the American economic system."

If you are between 20 and 30 years of age and you are willing to invest as little as $50 a month, we will provide the education, motivation and on-going support you will need to help you net over one million *dollars at retirement, or before. And even if the plan you select doesn't produce as much as we would hope, at least you should have far more than if you invested nothing.*

If you are over 30, depending on how much you are able to put aside each month, you too can achieve financial security.

*In any case, if you approve, we **will** help you attain financial freedom. We **will** lead the way for others to follow.*

Do you think you could handle that kind of compassion? You bet you could! How could it *not* have a positive impact on your productivity and your loyalty to the company?

But wait -- there are the scoffers who have been conditioned to believe they are losers and can never have what what they secretly dream of having: *Me, a millionaire? Me, save $50 a month? After I pay the rent, buy food, pay a couple of bucks on the credit card, rent a movie and do some shopping, I don't have enough money left over to buy a pot to piddle in, and you're telling me I can become a millionaire? Get real!*

By all means, let's get real. It may be impossible or difficult for some people, even a lot of people, but recent studies by the U.S. Census Bureau and the Rand Corporation show that the *typical* 16-to 19-year old girl spends $68 a *week* for items ranging from records to makeup. The truth is, you can save a lot more than you think you can. You just have to decide what's *really* important.

In addition to the scoffers, you can also hear the doubters: *What if I start investing my hard-earned money and the investment program goes sour. I'll loose everything.* That's a reasonable concern. But we're not suggesting that anyone invest anything other than what they would otherwise fritter away on lottery tickets, amusements and just plain "things" that aren't worth the money and will be forgotten soon after they've been purchased.

If you begin an investment program and something terrible happens to the economy, chances are you won't lose everything. If it's money you'd have spent on junk, you'd still lose, so why not go for it? You may end up with less than you hoped for, but isn't something better than nothing, which, as things stand now, is probably what you will have when you are 65? The point is, you, the American worker, deserve and have a right to keep at least a portion of what you earn and to turn it into more than you ever dreamed possible. And you *can* do it, particularly with the help of Corporate America!

America is still the land of oppportunity. There is absolutely no excuse for so much poverty and near-poverty. The freedom and means to amass money is staggering. What is also staggering is that so few people either don't realize this truth or don't know how to find and take advantage of the wealth-building opportunities.

Part of the reason for the "never get ahead" syndrome is the relentless pressure to buy everything and anything, whether or not it's needed or worthy of the price. We are constantly hyped into believing happiness is ours only if we spend everything we have. Which not only makes saving difficult, but unpopular.

It's time to let the cat out of the bag: Spending it all results in slavery. Saving and investing is the key to liberation. Never mind that you have little to save after you take care of your necessary expenses. You can always save something, and it is that "something", saved on a regular basis and invested wisely that will set you apart from the losers.

The good news is that a tremendous amount of help is available. You just have to discover where it is and learn how to make it work for you.

▶ 5 ◀

Getting Down
To The
Nitty Gritty

Hopefully, you now realize you don't have to live the rest of your life as a money slave, working your tail off for a paltry paycheck and then seeing it finessed out of your control and into the pockets of others who don't need the money nearly as much as you do. You've decided to pay off your credit cards, use them only in an emergency, or better yet, you've cut them up and thrown them away. You are going to hang on to as much of your hard earned money as possible and make it GROW FOR YOU.

As a result of your new awareness you've talked with and raised the consciousness of your co-workers, and all of you have developed a raging righteous anger about your financial situation if it is not what it ought to be. Not only are you feeling that anger, but you are determined to transform it into positive action. You are going to ask your company (and your union if there is one) to help set up an investment program.

How do you go about it? Go directly to the person or persons who are in a position to make decisions and explain that individually and as a group, you want to take control of your financial destiny but that you are going to need some and perhaps even a lot of help. (No snickering, please. So what if your company is cheap? You'll never know what you can get unless you ask.) Without being hostile, let them know that you mean business and that you won't be put off. Also let them know that you intend to "go public" with your plan. If the company greets your request for assistance with the attitude that "gee, we'd be happy to help -- why didn't we think of it first" assure them that such a response will merit good publicity. If the company tells you to get lost, that response will generate "appropriate" publicity.

Tell them you'd like the company to provide an independent non-salaried Director of Financial Freedom or whatever you want to call him or her for the specific purpose of implementing, coordinating and overseeing the necessary education, motivation and on-going support for employees who want to invest for their future security. Education could include, but not be limited to, regularly scheduled seminars, speakers, films, and easily understood educational materials. Motivation should be in the form of a visible, aggressive, supportive, on-going company policy toward the effort. The Director's compensation would be tied to how well employees benefit from his or her services. If they do well, the Director should do well, too. Nothing beats a win-win situation.

If the decision makers fly into a tizzy at the prospect of having to spend the piddling amount of money it would take to bring in a financial planner, ask to see a list of organizations or institutions that are beneficiaries of your company's philanthropy. You may be amazed and angry to learn that some of the profit you helped to create is given away to suspect causes with names like Save the Sand Fleas Foundation or the Coalition to Preserve Swamp Hogs. You may also find that some of the profit you helped to generate has been donated to political causes that are questionable. Let them know that those projects simply aren't as important as looking after the heart and soul of the business -- the employees.

While you are talking turkey to your bosses, let them know that pins, pens, pictures, watches, rocking chairs and the like are no longer acceptable rewards at retirement, particularly if they are the only tangible evidence that you ever worked for the company.

They're nice, of course, but they don't pay the bills.

IF ALL ELSE FAILS, TAKE THE BULL BY THE HORNS

If your company refuses to get the ball rolling, regardless of what you do to sway them, then be prepared to take the initiative. Here are some ideas:

Organize an enthusiastic-to-rabid battalion of co-workers. Ask for use of a company meeting room for strategy sessions. If management denies your request because it is scared out of its wits that you are plotting to destroy the company, try to get the community room at a bank or the library. Start talking with local bank officers, accountants, the Chamber of Commerce, Rotary, Lions -- anybody you feel could be of help. Who would they recommend as speakers or resource persons? Contact recognized financial planners and invite several of them to speak to your group. Ask them for specifics. What can they do for you? What kind of track record do they have? Will they give names of satisfied clients? If they beg off with "that's a personal matter between me and my clients" -- they are losers and you don't need them. Having tangible evidence of success is important because financial planners make their money selling financial products. It is possible that they may be more skilled at selling products than making money for their clients. The same goes for stock brokers who are always anxious to speak to groups. They are not in business primarily for *your* benefit. Ask if they can set up a program that will produce 20 percent annualized compounded growth over any five year period. If they tell you they can achieve such growth, ask how they do it, and demand to see hard evidence that they have indeed achieved that goal for others. If they claim they can make much more than 20 percent for you, be wary!

There is an alternative to the financial planner and others with products to sell. It's called "doing it yourself" using the expertise of others, such as that provided by financial expert Dick Fabian. He calls his method the "Fabian Compounding Goal" which has an impressive 10-year track record of attainment of 20 percent annualized compounded growth over any five year span. What makes his approach so appealing is that it is so simple. He monitors certain high performing mutual funds, and using indicators he has developed, determines when to be in or out of the stock market. Those who follow his plan were out of the stock market before the October 1987 crash.

Anyone can implement his system. An individual, a group, *or a company*.

Fabian insists that those who use his method first understand how it works. To that end he has developed a library of easy-to-understand materials. One item in particular should be obtained by the prospective investor and aspiring millionaire -- a manual and tape titled "Compounded Growth: Your Key to Wealth." The manual gives several examples of how various amounts of invested money will grow over a given period of time. Chances are you've never seen anything like it, and if it doesn't motivate you to start an investment program immediately, nothing will. What is particularly startling is that a mere $50 invested monthly over 30 years will yield over a million dollars providing it is allowed to grow at the 20 percent annualized growth rate. You say you don't want to wait 30 years? Or you don't think you could manage to save $50 a month? Then how about $25 a month? Would you be satisfied with over $28,000 in 15 years? Or almost $10,000 in 10 years? Just as a result of not throwing away $25 a month on some useless junk you won't remember you bought the next day?

For more information on the Fabian investment plan and available educational materials, write or call:

Telephone Switch Newsletter
P.O. Box 2538
Huntington Beach, CA 92647
1-800 843-8885
1-800 247-6496 in California

Fabian's system certainly isn't the only approach to investing. There are *many* ways to make money, including (but not limited to!) annuities, bonds, real estate partnerships and Single Premium Whole Life (SPWL) insurance products.

Purchase of a SPWL policy is one of the "hottest" ways of investing that has happened along in a long time. SPWLs are so hot in fact that the government is talking seriously about "putting a lid" on them -- in effect, making them less than the desirable investment instruments they are at the moment. If Congress does take action to eliminate the tax benefits, it is hoped that at least some of provisions that make them so attractive will remain in place. For example, it is expected that those who purchased a SPWL before a certain date will be able to retain the original benefits.

What makes them so exciting? Basically, the interest you realize with a SPWL is *tax free* at this time. Which means that if the earnings are left to compound, you could wind up with a sizeable amount of money in a relatively short period of time.

Let's say you purchase a SPWL for $5,000 and it earns 10 percent. Every seven years your money would double:

7	years:	$10,000
14	years	$20,000
21	years	$40,000
28	years	$80,000

Is that exciting? It should be, and it is! Ah, but you don't have $5,000? Not too many workers do. But how is your credit? Have you been working long enough and become credit-worthy enough to borrow the money? Are you reliable enough to pay back a $5,000 loan at the rate of $25 or $50 a month? You say you'd rather not borrow the money? How many times have you borrowed three times that much for a new car you really didn't need just yet, or perhaps you got a loan for a boat (even if it's just a canoe!) you only use during the summer? The big question is, do you love yourself enough to want to give yourself a gift of $80,000 in 28 years? If you live that long you will be working that long, so why not have *at least, if not more* than that to show for all the years you've worked? If you also make other kinds of investments, this could be the icing on the cake for you!

There are lots of different SPWL products available and you should begin right now to educate yourself about them. For more information contact:

Tina K. Baughman
President
Independent Advantage Financial
10960 Wilshire Blvd, Suite 2320
Los Angeles, CA 90024-3883
1-800-553-9181

As another way to go, employees may wish to pool their resources and have their money professionally managed. Generally it takes a minimum of $25,000 to get started. That's a lot of money, but 25 employees who can save $1,000 each would start the ball rolling.

However, before entering into any management agreement, participants should thoroughly investigate the firm's background and track record, always keeping in mind that risk, as well as profit, is always possible no matter how qualified and ethical a manager might be.

For the individual looking to get his feet wet fast with just small amounts of money, reputable investment newsletters can often provide excellent leads. For example, just about every issue of *Personal Finance*, (1101 King St., Ste. 400, Alexandria, VA 22314) discusses several sound investments you can buy into for very little money. One recent issue devoted an entire article to "Big Opportunities For The Little Guy" in which editor Richard Band offers several excellent wealth-building ideas for investors who might be considered "Pee Wee Leaguers." Noting that rising costs and a shortsighted rush for a quick buck explain why many financial institutions aren't interested in helping the little investor any more, Band insists that ". . . you don't have to take this tomfoolery lying down. If your're a small investor yourself, or you've got children or grandchildren in that category, you can still find plenty of top-performing vehicles for your money with low minimums and low overhead." To support that claim he discusses several money-making opportunities including one stellar mutual fund which will accept investments of any size, even 10 or 20 dollars!

As an extra benefit, *Personal Finance* subscribers are given names, addresses and phone numbers of reliable persons and companies that can be contacted.

Another highly respected newsletter to consider is *Donohue's Moneyletter* (P.O. Box 6640, Holliston, MA 01746) It's geared primarily to the buying and selling of mutual funds and money market funds. While it's not oriented to beginners, those who catch on quickly and are really serious about their finances will find it an excellent source of reliable information. William Donohue, editor of *Donohue's Moneyletter,* often provides well researched info on superior funds that can be gotten into with small amounts of money.

You might want to consider Mark Skousen's *Forecasts & Strategies* newsletter. (7811 Montrose Rd., Potomac, MD 20854) Skousen offers excellent leads and information of interest not just to people with big bucks, but to those just getting started. Really worthwhile.

Or try *Charles J. Givens Financial Digest* (921 Douglas Ave., Altamonte Springs, Fl 32714). Givens relies on tax strategies to build wealth. Very informative!

About newsstand money magazines: They're educational, but if you expect them to provide timely or "on target" investment advice, you may be disappointed. You'll get a better sense of what's going on by reading several newsletters published by those who can demonstrate a track record of success, such as those mentioned previously.

* * * *

These suggestions barely scratch the surface of the types and sources of information that are available to budding millionaires. Read and study as much as you can while you are saving the money you will need to get started. Then, when you are ready to invest, no matter how little it is, you will feel comfortable that you've made a wise decision. While it's important to get your investment program started as soon as possible, don't jump into anything that sounds too good to be true, because it probably is.

At the risk of being repetitious, let's be real clear about this: *If employees could get an investment program going on their own without corporate or other assistance it would be wonderful, but it's unrealistic. The negative influences that shape our thinking, values and habits relating to money and what we do with it, require aggressive counter measures. In order for an employee investment program to work, it will take dedicated, unstinting corporate involvement and support. Whatever a company agrees to do, it must be a high-profile effort that will generate employee enthusiasm, participation, public support and set an example for other companies to follow. Nothing less will do.*

EVEN "MOM AND POP" CAN HELP

So far, the emphasis has been on the moral responsibility of large corporations. But there is no reason why smaller companies could not rethink their attitude toward their employees. Even a small "mom and pop" operation that likely has *very* loyal employees could say, *Look, how would you guys like it if we called in a financial planner to help you invest for your future? We may never be big enough to provide you with a pension or other goodies but we do value your service and would like to give you tangible evidence of our appreciation. If we go under as a company, we don't want you to join the ranks of the homeless who gave years of dedicated service and suddenly found themselves unemployed and with nothing to fall back on. If the company manages to stay afloat we certainly don't want you to retire with just "fond memories" because they don't buy food, shelter and other necessities.* Ask any serious-minded employee if he would like free financial planning assistance and he will jump at the opportunity!

As a matter of fact, any organization can help its members in the same way. Churches, social, business and professional clubs -- whatever. For most people things are easier when done as a group. It's often tough for people to take individual action -- we've talked about that already. The point is, there is so much help available it is unthinkable not to take advantage of it.

In addition to financial planning assistance any company, regardless of size, can set up a "Simplified Employee Pension" also known as a "SEP." It's easy for an employer to do but it will require a tax-deductible contribution on the part of the company. The good news is that the company does not have to pay any consultant fees, commissions or administrative expenses to start and run a SEP. Best of all, it does not have to file any documents with the government. A really small business with 25 or fewer employees can set up a "Salary Reduction SEP" which is an employee savings plan and not a pension plan. The company makes no financial contribution, which is perfectly okay if the company simply can't afford an extra outlay of money.

You see, there just aren't any valid excuses for a company, regardless of size, not to do *something* to help employees build a solid financial future. For more information on SEPs, send $3.00 and a self-addressed stamped business size envelope to Pension Publications, Suite 704, 918 16th Street, N.W., Washington, D.C. 20006 and request a copy of "The Pension Plan Almost Nobody Knows About." It's easy to read and understand. Share it and discuss it with your co-workers then meet with your boss. He might not be aware of how easy it is to help you.

SHARING THE WEALTH PAYS OFF

What else can Corporate America do? More companies should consider implementing profit sharing. It could eliminate the need to bring in expensive motivational speakers or to set up time and money-consuming behavior modification programs designed to bolster productivity. For most people, knowing they own a "piece of the action" is a powerful incentive to do their best.

Furthermore, if workers are encouraged to invest the money they receive as a result of profit sharing, instead of taking it in cash, their net take could be substantially increased, and could serve as an even greater inducement to be maximally productive.

Companies that now have a profit sharing plan for managers and upper level people should consider extending it to lower level workers. When a manager gets a profit bonus based on the productivity of those he manages, but those who are the producers don't get anything extra -- *that's the absolute pits*! The analogy that immediately comes to mind is that of the farmer who uses a team of mules to pull his plough. The mules do all the work, in return for which they get food and water. That's very adequate compensation for the mules. And it's okay for the farmer to reap *all* the benefits of the animals' labor. However, it is despicable when men work for the equivalent of the mules' reward of food and water while the man who drives the laborers gets all the benefits. *Workers are not dumb animals, or "beasts of burden." They are human beings.*

Yes, the manager *should* receive profit sharing. His managerial and leadership skills are valuable to the company. But those who work under his direction are valuable to the company, too, and deserve to be rewarded accordingly.

Another benefit of profit sharing might show up in a reduction of internal theft. While profit sharing might not completely eliminate the problem, it could substantially reduce it if employees understood the extent to which theft cuts into the amount they could receive as profit-sharing. Honest employees would likely monitor less honest co-workers and not allow them to negatively impact the profit picture.

However, employees should not expect to share in profits when they are working for a company struggling for survival. Such companies could make it understood that if employees are willing to give their best during the lean years, they will profit handsomely down the line. When the company *does* begin to prosper, the promise should be kept. The good will generated by a kept promise would undoubtedly result in even greater profit for the company. In one way or another, the law of reciprocity never fails. What you sow, you will reap.

BACK TO THE BASICS: DO IT THE RIGHT WAY

Many companies are finding it necessary to provide remedial reading programs for workers. More companies should do it as a matter of policy to catch those marginal and non-readers who "fall through the cracks."

For a reading program to be truly successful the *right* approach must be used. Some corporate efforts are doomed to failure because the programs or methods used are the same as those used by the public schools. Which doesn't make sense since the schools failed their mission the first time around. Would a company re-hire an incompetent ex-employee to teach new employees how to do the job he messed up? If a company is serious about providing reading and other basic skills it will not use public school materials or personnel to administer or teach the programs, unless there is a proven track record of success.

The reading method of choice in most public schools is based on "whole word recognition" also called "look-say" or memorization. This means the child's reading ability is limited to the number of words he can memorize. (This method was originally used to teach deaf children because they couldn't hear sounds. That it is used to teach hearing children amounts to imposing a handicap on them.) The only method that produces consistently successful results is *intensive phonics*. By learning the sounds of combinations of letters and vowels that make up words, the student learns to "decode" words; he then has the ability to read an unlimited number of words. Sound simple? It is, and it works. But you'd never know it by the way the method is criticized by some so-called reading experts.

There are several excellent phonics programs. One that is particularly successful is called *Professor Phonics*, developed by Sr. Monica Foltzer, M.Ed., an experienced educator with an impressive track record of success, even with children said to suffer from a reading disorder called dyslexia. All the materials needed for the *Professor* Phonics program are supplied in a "kit" and are available for under $20. Without question, it is the best organized, most effective, simplest and least expensive system on the market. For full details, write to:

> S.U.A. Phonics
> 1339 East McMillan St.
> Cincinnati, OH 45206

An employer wishing to set up a reading program using the intensive phonics approach will need to hire a qualified phonics teacher, and that will cost the company money, but so what? The cost would be a mere drop in the corporate bucket, which may be overflowing for any number of questionable causes not related to employee benefits.

There are many excellent phonics teachers. To contact one in your area write to Sr. Monica Foltzer at the address above, or:

> Reading Reform Foundation
> 949 Market Street, Suite 436
> Tacoma, WA 98402
> (206) 572-9966

or:

> Mrs. Ann Herzer,
> 5239 N. 70th Place,
> Paradise Valley, AZ 85253.

Mrs. Herzer is a certified reading specialist who could provide an employer with the expertise needed to set up a program that would give employees (or anyone else) the skills needed to read in just weeks.

* * * *

What Corporate America should and could be doing for employees is so basic, you really have to wonder why it should be necessary to make an issue of it. But because we are all imperfect, even the best intentioned among us sometimes *need to be told* what we ought to be doing.

Old age is right around the corner for *all of us*. With very little time and money, Corporate America could and *must* help employees turn that corner with dignity and the peace of mind that comes with financial security.

Young workers can preview their future by looking at the dismal circumstances of many of today's elderly who have worked and saved all their lives, and in spite of their thrift, are experiencing financial devastation.

The future for many of today's workers will not be pleasant. There will be less money available to pay for the level of medical care that today's elders take for granted. Cost containment advocates and "death with dignity" measures will determine who should live and for how long.

What to do? The solution isn't more government intervention in our lives and finances.

Part of the solution is better financial planning and restraint on the part of those forces that shape the perception of what is needed to be happy. There must be more balance and fairness in the messages that are directed at young workers. To the degree that they are conned into spending everything they earn and then some, it is imperative that they be helped and encouraged to save and invest while there is still time. It could revolutionize the quality of life for so many Americans and have a dynamic, civilizing influence on society as a whole.

▸ 6 ◂

Old Age: It's Gonna Getcha -- Count On It!

If you belong to a union, your representative *may* be an invaluable ally in getting an investment program started. But don't count on it. If unions were truly dedicated to getting workers the best benefits possible, investment planning would have become "the norm" long ago.

This observation is not meant to denigrate the value of unions. Membership dues enable the union to negotiate an array of important benefits paid by your employer: Periodic cost of living increases; a good or not-so-good retirement plan; on-the-job perks such as mandatory rest periods, free food and uniforms; at least partial payment for a variety of medical services -- major or minor surgery, prescriptions, dental and vision care; discounts on tickets to games and amusement parks; special prices on furniture, cars and other big ticket items. Many of the above are critical to families raising children and trying to make ends meet.

As much help as those day-to-day "here and now" goodies are when you get them, if they stop at retirement, where will you be? Will your pension take up the slack? Will it generously pay for all your food, living, entertainment, travel, and medical expenses? Will there be enough money to pay a couple of hundred dollars or more a month for an insurance policy that will provide extended nursing home care some time in the near or distant future? Or will it pay the bills for an expensive, lingering illness while you are at home? Chances are you will need more than what your pension will pay for -- a lot more. The cost of living is going in one direction: UP.

Unions must begin to negotiate packages that include more than "here and now" benefits and pension plans. Unions must see to it that employees are helped to create a real financial cushion that will take the worry and pain out of retirement. Again, we're not talking handouts; we're talking about financial planning assistance for employees.

Even if you think you are set with the best pension plan going, what will happen if your company is taken over and the new owners confiscate the funds the former owner set aside for your retirement? *It happens.* If you are counting on that money and you are close to retirement when the bomb drops, what will you do? You won't worry too much if during the past 20-30 years you regularly socked a modest chunk of your income into a solid investment program. (Thanks, perhaps, to the help of a crack financial planner the union might have negotiated for you, at very little cost to the company?) You may not have what you thought you'd have, but you will still be well taken care of.

Or your company may decide to change the retirement plan after you've been there for 15 years, which will leave you with something at retirement, but far less than you expected. This, too, happens, and will become more common as more companies try to find ways to cut operating expenses.

Okay, even if your pension goes down the tubes, your children will take care of you. Really? What assurance do you have that they will be in a financial position to do so, even if you stay healthy as a horse? They have their own families and lives to live. Even if they could, would they welcome you into their home, particularly if you've been less than an ideal parent? If you are childless will relatives want to take care of you? Why should they? What have you ever done for them?

Ah, but the government will take care of you! After all, there is Social Security and Medicare! *What fools we mortals be.* Let's talk about Social Security and Medicare, just a little. Don't go away -- it won't be boring.

THE HOAX CALLED "SOCIAL SECURITY"

You may not know it but there is nothing secure about Social Security. It was never meant to replace prudent personal financial planning. When Social Security was being debated in Congress in 1935 our lawmakers deluded themselves into believing that workers would never have to ante up more than $90 a year. That's because the purpose (then) was merely to augment private pensions, to provide the aged with a "floor of subsistence" and to prevent suffering. So here we are in the 1990s with retirees and disabled persons getting Social Security "benefits" and living not much better than alley cats who must dig in garbage cans for their daily sustenance. And we still believe that when the present generation of workers retires there will be enough to keep them living in the style to which they have become accustomed?

If you don't remember anything else you read in this book, remember this: *Old age is not a TV drama that ends in 60 minutes. It's real, and if you haven't prepared for it, each day may be a living hell. You will look back and curse the time and money you wasted chasing meaningless fun and games, refusing to think about and plan for the future.*

By the time you are ready to claim everything that had been taken out of your paycheck, and it will have been plenty, the money may not be there for you. The tax taken out of your paycheck goes into the general fund to meet current needs, and as everyone knows, there are an awful lot of elderly and disabled people out there, and the situation isn't getting better. Oh, you've read about a Social Security surplus that's guaranteed to take care of everything for everybody for at least the next 100 years? ("Social Security Surpluses Loom," *Los Angeles Times*, April 2, 1988) Do you also believe in the tooth fairy?

If you also believe there is pie in the sky, consider this: In 1966 Social Security paid $255 for burial expenses. In 1988 Social Security paid $255 for burial expenses. Has your dog died recently? Was $255 enough to bury it? And you trust the government when it says there is or will be enough to take care of you when you retire or become disabled? Even as newspapers are filled with reassuring stories about all the money in the non-existent Social Security fund, Federal Reserve Chairman Alan Greenspan has asked Congress to consider trimming Social Security and other entitlement programs as a means to reduce the federal budget deficit. ("Greenspan Urges Cut in Social Security Program," *Los Angeles Times*, March 3, 1988)

Because the birthrate continues to decline due to infertility, more women opting to have abortions, or choosing to remain childless, those who are working will have to be taxed astronomically to keep benefits flowing. In 1947 there were 22 workers for every beneficiary. By 1972 there were only three. (*Washington Bulletin*, October 14, 1974) Does that tell you something about how much you will have to kick into the system if you are a young worker? How much Social Security tax can be extracted from too few productive members of society to pay for care for too many elderly, without reducing everyone to poverty? Is there no limit to the load America's active work force will accept before it rebels and demands an end to what is nothing more than a fraud, swindle, highway robbery or whatever else you want to call it?

Good grief, did we make a naughty suggestion? Dump Social Security? Clearly, we can't abruptly drop the Social Security System. If in fact we had the guts to do it at all, it would have to be phased out so that those who currently depend on the meager benefits wouldn't be left totally destitute, and those who have already paid in could be reimbursed.

Easy? No. Possible? Yes. If American workers and our lawmakers were not so deeply imbued with socialistic myopia, they'd understand the necessity of at least amending the Social Security Act to place it on a sound actuarial insurance basis, or better still, transferring it to private insurance companies and permitting individual citizens to provide for their own security and protection of their families.

You can hear the detractors of private initiative: "Oh, people wouldn't contribute to a private program." Are you allowed to drive a vehicle without having proof of insurance? We are required by law to do and pay for all kinds of things for "our own good." Does every worker have to file an income tax return? The law could require that every worker must show evidence on his return that he does have his own "social security" plan. And it would cost us a lot less than what is being taken out of our paychecks. Just think -- that 7.51 percent matching contribution made by your employer could be turned over to you, or better yet, just eliminated because as everybody knows, the tax that the employer pays is passed on to the consumer in the form of higher prices for goods and services.

Politicians call for "reform" of the Social Security system but their idea of reform means more withholding tax, higher taxes in general and extending the age of retirement to 67 and beyond. What a tragedy these politicians have nothing better to offer our young people than dehumanizing nostrums guaranteed to keep them in financial bondage and dependent on the government.

Real reform has been offered over the years by many astute economics experts and folks with just plain common sense. For example, in 1971 President Nixon wanted Congress to allow "do-it-yourself" pension plans to supplement Social Security benefits. He was on the right track but his idea fell on deaf Congressional ears. His proposal was designed to help those workers who weren't covered by a company-financed or union-negotiated plan. According to the plan, a 40-year-old worker who put in $1,500 for 25 years could have an annual income of $7,500 on top of Social Security payments. While that amount is nice, in today's economy, and likely in any future economy, that amount really doesn't buy a lot of medication or take care of daily living expenses for very long. But give him credit for wanting to do *something* constructive.

Under his proposal a worker would have been required to deposit his contribution into a savings account or in a mutual fund or other forms of securities. (*Chicago Daily News*, December 8, 1971) In essence, this is similar to what is proposed in this book, but with one major difference: The government must not be involved, other than requiring a private plan and allowing a tax deduction for the money saved or invested. To be successful, *it must be a private sector initiative!* And that's where Corporate America has a golden opportunity to show off its leadership capability and social conscience.

The government is really bent on making and keeping us poor and dependent. Look how Congress has effectively destroyed the usefulness of IRAs (Individual Retirement Accounts). For a lot of people, putting money into an IRA as a tax advantaged retrirement vehicle no longer makes sense. Yes, the government gives, and just as soon as it can, takes it back and then some.

THE GOVERNMENT IS A NIGGARDLY NURSEMAID

As for Medicare, even now the government is hard-pressed financially to take care of the needs of those on Medicare, also known as latent socialized medicine which has never worked to anyone's satisfaction any place it has been tried. All you need do is look at the dismal socialized health care system in England, which ironically, our government is striving to copy, in spite of the glaring inadequacies. For example, the London *Daily Telegraph* of April 1, 1985 (that's correct -- 1985) reported that prescription charges were going to rise 25 percent and "doctors will be required to prescribe from a limited list of medicines." A total of 1,800 drugs in seven categories -- indigestion remedies, laxatives, painkillers, cough remedies, tonics, vitamins and tranquilizers were withdrawn. Of course, doctors could still prescribe the banned drugs privately but patients would have to pay full cost for them. It's the same old story. Either you take care of your own needs or they may not get taken care of at all.

If the AIDS epidemic continues to explode and the government is forced to pick up the tab for the care of AIDS patients -- treatment that is often prolonged and costly -- will the government be able to raise enough money through taxes to pay for its role as National Nursemaid? Assuming you don't acquire AIDS, you may still develop some other life-threatening condition such as cancer. Wouldn't it be comforting to know you had the means to pay for the best care available? There is recently enacted federal legislation to provide for the cost of treating incurable or lingering illnesses. Let's take a look at the highlights of this "wonderful gift" from the gods in Washington who like to run our lives and play Robin Hood with our money:

Senior citizens will be hit with a 15 percent surcharge on their tax bill in 1989. By 1993 this tax which has been disguised as a "supplemental Medicare premium" will rise to 28 percent. By 2005, it is estimated that the extra tax on a couple 65 or older will be nearly $8,000 a year. *Such a bargain!?* The reality is that 90 percent of the beneficiaries of this *compulsory* insurance are now getting similar benefits from private insurance, former employers or government programs. The remaining 10 percent could get a whole lot more through private insurance.

What this "wonderful gift" also means is that 40 percent of the elderly who pay federal income taxes will be carrying the load for the approximately 18 million seniors who have no taxes to pay. In effect, it's just one more reworked socialistic redistribution of wealth that discriminates against the middle-class elderly. Once again, the "haves" will be zapped to take care of the "have-nots." And the government has the monumental arrogance to lead the public, particularly the elderly, to believe that they are getting something for nothing. The real irony in this situation is that two of the most erstwhile champions of senior citizens, the AARP (American Association of Retired Persons) and Senator Claude Pepper supported the charade. These days, it's tough to tell who your true friends really are!

Lest anyone think the above is an unjust appraisal of the situation, it should be noted that even former President Reagan has expressed concern about potential runaway expenses of providing new benefits. Said Reagan, "We have no real way of knowing how much these services will cost." He also warned that a jump in expenses "could be more than a budget problem, it could be a tragedy. The program, after all, is to be paid for by the elderly themselves. So we must control the costs of these new benefits, or we'll harm the very people we're trying to help." ("President Signs Bill Expanding Medicare Aid," *Los Angeles Times*, July 2, 1988)

Recall, back in 1935, when it was projected the Social Security tax would never exceed $90 a year?

Remember former President Reagan's prophetic words: "We have no real way of knowing how much these services will cost." We can't say we haven't been warned!

EXPECT TO DIE SOONER THAN LATER

Many hospitals are starting to take a "cost effective" approach to the provision of care and services. Committees, not individual physicians, now decide if continuation of a particular treatment or service can be financially justified for a particular patient. As medical care becomes more socialized and quality of care declines, we can expect to see doctors and hospitals forced to make many harsh "life or death" decisions. Which means that treatment and services now considered "ordinary" will become "extraordinary" and not available to all patients under all circumstances.

At this time physicians still more or less make an effort to keep the ailing elderly alive as long as possible -- even when it becomes clear that death is near. For now, but to a diminishing extent, it's considered "ordinary" treatment -- the reflection of an ethic long held by physicians and nurses that life is precious and worthy of care and preservation. However, when it becomes necessary to implement "cost effective" treatment, when money becomes more important than preservation of life, then "pulling the plug," disconnecting the respirator, and even withholding food and water, are easily justified.

The reality of such a scenario was addressed by columnist Nat Hentoff in *The Washington Post*, March 26, 1988. According to Hentoff, a proposal that could shorten the lives of millions of Americans has been proposed by Daniel Callahan, director of the Hastings Center, a "think tank" that examines ethical issues. Callahan is disturbed by the precipitous rise in the cost of medical care, particularly for the elderly. He wants laws enacted that would prevent the elderly beyond a certain age from receiving Medicare payments for certain forms of open heart surgery and extended stays in an intensive care unit. If a chronic vegetative state existed, feeding tubes would be removed. He wants the elderly to accept "a reasonable, tolerable natural life span." Isn't that what we all want? The question is, what would be Callahan's definition or the government's definition of "a reasonable, tolerable natural life span," particularly when the government doesn't have enough money to go around? Wouldn't a proposal such as his gain swift legitimacy when there are so many competing demands for money -- such as daycare for young families? Or for AIDS research? After all, as the thinking goes, aren't young people more important and more valuable than the elderly who have had their shot at life? Remember President Reagan's warning that "we must control the costs of these new benefits. . . " That's an ominous message that mustn't be sloughed off as mere political rhetoric. Not just the elderly, but those coming up right behind them have now been set up to accept a new utilitarian, money-driven ethic based on a yet to be defined "reasonable, tolerable, natural life span."

Bye, bye, grandma. We love you but we don't have the money to keep you around much longer and the government says you have had a "reasonable, tolerable, natural life span." That our lives are enriched by your presence doesn't matter. It's just not cost effective to keep you alive.

Interestingly enough, Callahan concedes that those of the elderly who do not depend on Medicare would be free to pay for whatever they wanted. Now, guess what? Under that "wonderful" new federal law referred to above, the patient is still responsible for charges in excess of the fees recommended by Medicare.

Not too far into the future, we can expect that more ailing people will be "allowed" or even "assisted" to expire sooner than later. However, if you have enough money to pay for quality care, you may escape the grim reaper and cost conscious "death with dignity" advocates a while longer. When given adequate care and treatment, sick people, even elderly people, do recover from seemingly terminal illnesses and go on to lead fulfilling lives that meet *their own* standards.

Radical proposals of the type made by Daniel Callahan, even if not taken seriously by the general public, do open discussion and plant the seed for future action. Even now we can see that he has made an "acceptable" proposal. For example, an investigation made by the U.S. Department of Health and Human Services has determined that the federal government spends about $2 billion a year on unnecessary hospital care for Medicare patients. Back problems, diabetes and upper respiratory infections are among the most common sources of questionable admissions, according to the findings. As another example, an elderly patient with chest pain and shortness of breath might be on the verge of suffering a heart attack -- or he might have indigestion from a spicy meal. If a doctor orders the patient admitted to a hospital and there is no serious problem, that would be classified as an unnecessary admission. Action to reduce "unnecessary admissions to hospitals is one of the most effective ways of saving Medicare dollars," the report said. ("Unnecessary Medicare Treatment Costs Put at $2 Billion," *Los Angeles Times,* May, 1988) You can bet on it!

How would you like it if your doctor, under pressure to keep down admissions, decided that *y*our chest pain was caused by indigestion but in fact, was a heart attack in progress from which you didn't recover? Does it matter? You're going to be dead anyway!

It bears repetition: In the future, the key to whether you are given the best medical care available or you are assisted into your grave by a penny pinching "death with dignity" committee or relatives who are tired of putting up with you (particularly if your expensive illness has made you cranky and difficult to live with) will be determined by whether or not *you* can pay for *your* care and treatment. *Money matters.* Particularly when it's badly needed and you don't have it.

YOU CAN'T AFFORD
TO BE SICK
RIGHT NOW...

Even if you are not sick enough to require hospitalization, just getting a prescription filled at your pharmacy can be a painful experience right now.

Fortunately, at least at this time, many workers have a company-paid "prescription plan" that enables them to pay just a few dollars for medication that otherwise would mean macaroni and cheese every night at least until next payday. That's the good news. The bad news is that because of skyrocketing costs of doing business, many prescription plan providers are imposing "cost containment" measures. (Shades of Jolly Old England in 1985! A replay is in the making in the U.S. and we don't even have full-blown socialized medicine yet!) Limitations are being placed on medications a plan will pay for, or the amount the plan will pay. There may be a requirement that the "generic" equivalent of a drug, which is less expensive, must be dispensed. (What is a "generic" drug? For example, "Motrin" is a brand name for "Ibuprofen" which is the generic name for Motrin. Any drug manufacturer can make Ibuprofen and give it any brand name they choose. The point is, it's all supposed to be "Ibuprofen.")

The problem with generics is that they may not always be the *exact* equivalent of their brand name counterparts. As this is written has media has uncovered a "scandal" in generic medications. It has been alleged that some generic drug manufacturers are turning out suspect products, and that some generic drugs may be dangerous to take. How accurate are the stories? Only a full scale investigation will tell. And even if such an investigation takes place, will the outcome change anything? One thing *is* certain. The publicity is causing quite a bit of panic, particularly among seniors. On some days the phone in the pharmacy just about rings off the hook with apprehensive questions. "I'm taking generic XYZ medication. Is it safe? How do I know it's safe? I don't feel so good. Do you think it's the generic drug I'm taking?" As a result, consumers are starting to demand brand name medication, even when the generic equivalent is working just fine. Some brand name drugs cost as much as four times as much as the generic, which a lot of seniors just can't afford unless their insurance will pay. Another thing is certain: manufacturers of brand name drugs must be getting dizzy seeing dollar signs in front of their eyes. The controversy can only have a positive impact on the corporate profit picture.

Unfortunately, even with the best generics -- and many are made by the same companies that manufacture brand name drugs -- some patients claim generic drugs don't produce the same results as the brand name drugs, or that they produce undesirable side effects. Whether the problem is real or imaginary, if a patient has difficulty with an inexpensive generic drug, and his prescription plan will not pay for the brand name equivalent which may be very expensive what choice does he have? That's right, he's going to pay for it himself or do without. This is just the beginning of what young people have to look forward to when they are seniors unless they have the means to pay their own way for care and services that the present generation of seniors still takes for granted.

Every working day I see countless withered and pained faces at the prescription counter. The sparkle of youth and health has left their eyes, replaced with the dead-fish dullness of glaucoma and cataracts. You have to be a hard-hearted old junkyard dog not to feel what they are feeling when they must pay $30 for a tiny bottle of eye drops to control their glaucoma *and* $80 for a month's supply of blood pressure medication *and*

$60 for arthritis tablets and maybe another $150 (that's right $150.00) for ulcer medication. For many seniors, their monthly pharmacy bill is much higher, even though they may be getting lower-priced generic medication. And the dignity-destroying 10 percent "senior citizens discount" which they have been trained to beg for doesn't help a heck of a lot.

The anguish caused by insufficient income and insurance is truly difficult to describe and many times you just can't find the right words to comfort these unfortunate people. As a matter of fact, there are no words of comfort when there simply isn't enough money to cover necessities. You don't know the meaning of ugly, mean and nasty until you've encountered a retired senior citizen who needs medication and can't afford it. It brings out the worst in many of them, as it probably would in most of us in the same situation. Even when they are too proud or civilized to curse and swear at you, you can sense their ill-concealed rage. It's obvious what they are thinking: *One more godawful decision has to be made about how to allocate this month's income -- should I buy all the medication, try to do without or cut back, or buy less food?* This kind of painful decision making goes on in spite of careful money management and shopping around for the best prices. Yes, you do experience the desperation that grips these senior citizens, and it's not pleasant. You wouldn't want to be in their shoes.

These are people from a generation who were taught to find pride in being independent and self-sufficient. Only lazy good-for-nothings accepted government "relief." They worked all their lives, raised a family and were good citizens. They retired from a company that provided them with a meager "retirement plan" and they figured that between their savings nest egg, the "retirement plan" and Social Security they would be able to live their remaining years in dignity. Then the rude awakening hit: Inflation and the demons of old age suddenly appeared. They didn't figure that taming high blood pressure or dealing with cataracts or trying to abate the pain of arthritis would cost so much. Those who might not be too proud to accept a handout are caught in the middle. They have too much income to qualify for government assistance but not enough to make ends meet. Yet another side to the coin is that those who have private insurance are finding the cost of paying the premiums for the coverage they need is becoming prohibitive.

Please don't make the mistake of thinking high prescription prices mean the pharmacy is getting rich at your expense. Nothing could be further from the truth. The high cost of a prescription begins long before your pharmacist enters the picture. The price the pharmacy must pay to stock medication leaves room for only the slimmest profit margin. Fierce competition between pharmacies, particularly in densely populated urban areas, keeps profits to a bare minimum. Just doing some comparison shopping will prove it.

Competition squeezes profit to such an extent that most pharmacies are forced to offer "loss leaders." These are often maintenance medications, such as those that lower blood pressure or regulate the heart. They are priced at below cost with the expectation that the bargain will lure you into the store. There is also the additional expectation that once you are in the store you will do a lot of impulse shopping for items with a mark-up that is high enough to offset the loss on the prescriptions used as a "loss leader." Really, it's not much different that going to the supermarket "just for a dozen eggs" that's on special and coming out with a basket laden with non-essential goodies. Unless you understand how the system works, and you can withstand the many temptations that surround you while you wait to get your "bargain" prescription, you will wind up on the losing end of the deal. A greater profit may be made on a $10 cosmetic item than on a $60 prescription, and for some pharmacies, it's the sale of such high-profit non-competitive "impulse" items that enables them to stay in business. *The cost of doing business is always paid by somebody.* It's a game that few consumers win.

Young people have a tendency to think they will never be sick or old. Even those not so young fall into that trap, particularly if they are in good health and enjoying life. If you are in that category, please do yourself a favor and take your head out of the sand. Even if you are zealously taking care of your health there are many diseases that don't discriminate. Even the best cared for Mercedes eventually needs expensive repairs. And even if you manage to stay in good health for an extended period of time, you never know when heredity will kick in and give you a swift shove downhill, at a rate that is faster than you could imagine.

Even if you are lucky enough to reach your golden years in relatively great shape, wouldn't it be nice to have enough money to live the way you really want to live?

Yes, old age is gonna getcha. Count on it! Whether it is a happy or painful time of your life very much depends on whether or not you start to prepare for it while you are young and healthy.

How much will you need to retire in style and comfort?

As much as you can possibly have. You can never be too well-fixed in your retirement.

If you don't spend it all during your lifetime, you can leave it to your children and grandchildren, or set up a trust for the money to be used for a worthwhile non-family cause. Like providing scholarships; buying books or equipment for a favorite private educational institution; or making it possible for a hospital or church to care for the needs of children or the elderly. The possibilities are endless.

What is so incredible is that having enough money to do good after you are gone is not all that difficult. It just takes knowledge, guts and determination. Mostly, determination.

7

How Much Will You Need?

How much will you need at retirement to live the way you want to live? No one except you could make that determination. You have to take into consideration all your probable sources of income: A pension, your savings, Social Security and any investments you may have made, then factor into that the likelihood of inflation and the probable cost of treating a catastrophic illness, and go from there.

It's certainly not easy to figure out what you'll need but a general "guesstimate" has been made by Richard E. Band, a Chartered Financial Analyst, in an article titled "Retirement Savings: How Much Is Enough?" It is reprinted below from *Personal Finance*, April 13, 1988, with permission from KCI Communications, Inc. (1988 copyright), 1101 King St., Suite 400, Alexandria, VA 22314; $118/year. If what has been said in the preceding pages isn't enough to spur you into action to start planning for your financial future, then surely this will:

Retirement Savings: How Much Is Enough?

Richard E. Band

One of the questions I'm frequently asked on the lecture circuit is, "How much money do I need to retire comfortably?" It's a simple question, but alas -- there's no simple answer. Without writing a book on the subject, let me raise a couple of issues that you ought to consider.

To begin with, it's important to recognize that Social Security benefits aren't going to put you on Easy Street. As a rule of thumb, Social Security benefits replace only about a third of a married worker's income (less if you're making more than about $50,000). Financial planners generally figure that a family needs 60 to 80 percent of its gross pre-retirement income to maintain its standard of living after retirement.

Take the case of a family with one breadwinner who earned $40,000 last year and retired at age 65 on January 1, 1988. Assuming the nonworking spouse is still alive, this family will receive approximately $13,680 from Social Security this year. Fourteen grand is quite a comedown when you've been living on forty.

Granted, many employees can look forward to company pension benefits. A good pension plan may replace another 30 percent or so of a worker's earnings -- if the worker has stayed with the company for several decades. But even then, with Social Security and your pension, you'll just barely squeak by. Who wants to scrimp and scrape when you could be jetting around to visit the grandchildren or sailing the seven seas?

Start Saving Now

The only way to assure yourself a comfortable retirement is to start saving -- and I mean now, regardless of your age. Even people in their 20s who are just entering the work force should begin setting aside something for retirement. In fact, the earlier you begin, the less you need to set aside each year.

When, Not How

Getting into a regular savings program early is far more important than how you invest the money. If you give your savings time to grow, you can pile up a sizable sum without being an investment genius. It isn't necessary to make a killing in the market or shoot for quick 10-to-1 gains.

"But how much should I put away?" you ask. The following table may help you come up with a reasonable guesstimate. In putting together these numbers, I've made the following assumptions:

▶ Inflation will average 4 percent from now until your retirement.

▶ Your salary is $20,000 today if you're 25 years old, $30,000 if you're 35 years old and $40,000 if you're 45 or older. As you mature, your salary will bump you up to these levels in dollars of today's purchasing power and will end at $40,000 (in real dollars).

▶ You can earn 8 percent a year, tax deferred until retirement, on your savings through an IRA, Keogh, 401(k) plan, annuity or other device.

▶ You'll retire married at age 65 and Social Security will replace one-third of your income.

▶ You want to maintain your income in retirement at no less than 60 percent of your final working year's salary (in dollars of constant purchasing power).

▶ You and your spouse will live 20 years after your retirement.

▶ You don't work for a company with a pension plan.

Get all that? Well, I never said it would be easy! But given all these 'simplifying' assumptions, here's the percentage of your gross income that you'll need to save each year -- for retirement purposes only -- from now until the day you walk out the factory gate for the last time:

Age	% of annual income saved	Projected final year's salary	Total nest egg at age 65
25	5.2	$192,040	$748,612
35	7.7	129,735	505,735
45	12.6	87,645	341,656
55	29.5	59,210	207,736

Don't let the figure in the last column scare you -- too much. A 35-year-old retiring in 30 years will need a minimum of half a million dollars to live comfortably. But remember, I'm building in a 4 percent inflation factor. That's why I inserted the final year's salary: your earnings (we hope) will be going up over the next 30 years along with the cost of living.

The general message from the chart is that it's easy to save enough for retirement *if you start early*. A 5 percent cut out of a young person's paycheck is a pittance.

On the other hand, people who wait until their 50s or 60s to begin thinking about retirement have waited too long. By then, there isn't enough time for the "miracle of compound interest" to work in your favor.

A married person who retired January 1 after making $40,000 last year will need an estimated $155,932 in savings to keep up his household's standard of living over the next 20 years. If you haven't socked that much away, I hope you've got richer relatives than I do to move in with.

* * * *

Read and re-read Mr. Band's article until you are able to apply the figures and his excellent advice to your situation. And please take note of his belief, which concurs with a basic premise of this book, that it's easy to save for a substantial retirement *if you start early*. The problem is, starting early is difficult. When you're on a limited income trying to put aside even a tiny sum is often downright painful. But it's not nearly as difficult as one might imagine. Every day, many of us let slip through our fingers what we call "pocket change." A dollar here, a dollar there. Let me tell you a little story that may elicit a snicker, but it says something important about the value of "pocket change" that we lose and never miss.

A couple of years ago my husband and I started picking up money from the street. When we first began this frugal practice, we'd put a found coin in our pocket and not give it another thought. As we began to realize the nickels, dimes, quarters, and even dollars (6 of them, one at a time) were mounting in value, we put aside what we found. To date, the "treasure" is about $70. One day at the Post Office I bent over to pick up a dime. A grizzly chap passing by caught the action and jeered, "That'll get you rich." I wonder if that same Old Boy who may be straining to make ends meet every month would like to have someone hand him $70 in one lump sum! We've decided to invest it in a (currently) top performing mutual fund mentioned in *Personal Finance*. There is no minimum amount needed to buy into the fund. We'll continue to add to the account with additional "street money". Since we don't want to burden the nice folks at this fund with trifling amounts, we'll wait until we find another five dollars worth of change.

The moral of this story? Start a "pocket change" kitty. Put your loose change into it every day and see how quickly you can get your investment program underway. And don't put it off. This very day begin to take action on behalf of your best friend -- you!

Those who say "money doesn't matter" are either lying or naive.

Having money means having peace of mind and freedom. Freedom to live as you will; freedom from the indignity of debt and waiting on the pleasure of others.

Money is power. In the hands of decent people it can be a force to bring about positive social and personal change.

When you need it and don't have it, life can be sheer hell. Ask the hungry and homeless.

In 1758 Benjamin Franklin said, "If you would know the value of money, go and try to borrow some."

Bankers and money lenders love debt. It makes them wealthy. It gives them freedom and power.

"Money doesn't matter"?

Really?

8

Just in Case
You Missed
The Message

If you're in the habit of reading just the first and last chapters of a book, you are "somewhat" in luck because this is "somewhat" of a summary of the preceding pages. But if you begin reading here you'll miss some critical hard-nosed "consciousness raising" that is absolutely essential to getting a handle on your financial situation. Reading just this section is like eating a fast-food lunch when you could be feasting on a seven-course dinner. You'll miss some tasty morsels. So please, *read it all.*

Specifically, the basic premise of the book is that everyone who works for a living -- especially those who are *not* self-employed -- *can* and *should* retire in a financial condition that will enable them to live the way they want to live. While it is intended for all workers, it is particularly for those in their twenties, thirties and forties -- those who still have the gift of time -- their wealth-building years. If the time value of these years is harnessed and intelligently put to work they can be truly magical years. But very few young workers are aware of the power in these years and tragically waste this precious time. This book provides the awareness that will enable workers to sieze their once-in-a-lifetime opportunity and use it to build their future financial security.

Building a secure financial future must begin with the understanding of a harsh basic reality: We are all victims of an exploitive work-and-spend ethic that promises far more than it can possibly deliver. Some of us deal with it better than others. Unfortunately, those who can least afford the exploitation -- those at or near the bottom of the pay scale -- are hurt the most. A constant barrage of compelling messages and enticing fantasies that promise "This is the good life and you can have it all if you will just spend every last dime you have, and then some" keeps them securely buckled in their seats at the back of our society's economic bus. *Just hand them their paycheck, wind them up, turn them loose, and they will predictably and quickly put their earnings back into circulation.* They serve as little more than perpetual motion machines that are programmed to keep the economy afloat. That's pretty much the totality of the perceived value of workers, and it stinks. They may as well be mules pulling a plough. *Think about it.*

A low-income worker caught in the "work and spend" trap might dream about having a lot of money, but believing he's being realistic, he spends the discretionary portion of his income on whatever pleasure he can find "here and now." Usually, there is adequate food, clothing, shelter, entertainment and sex, *so why fight the system?* His "investment plan" for the future is the weekly purchase of $10 or more of lottery tickets. No one has bothered to tell him that his chances of becoming a millionaire are greater if he saves and invests that money on a regular basis for the next 30 years.

Many workers who are a little higher on the pay scale are usually no better off. They're in the back of the same economic bus, but perhaps just two seats in front of their lower paid brothers and sisters. Their income provides them with enough money to play "let's pretend." Which means they are living beyond their means, going into debt to acquire all the trappings of the media-manufactured version of the "good life."

Human nature being what it is, when you've been conditioned to want it all but you know deep down in your gut that the possibility of having it all is not realistic, you tend to settle for as many "things" as you can get. Accumulation of material things is evidence you're "making it." And you play the "if only" game that feeds the need to spend more and more -- a deadly game that grinds you deeper into debt. *If only I could afford the payments on a flashy sports car I'd be somebody! If only I could get a higher spending limit on my credit card I could buy better clothes and I'd feel better about myself and maybe get a better job. If only I could afford to live in a better neighborhood I might meet a rich guy. If only. . . If only. . . .*

But acquiring "things" is *not* "making it." "Puttin' on the ritz" with a leased Mercedes while you can't pay the rent on time; wearing expensive clothes while running around in torn underwear or holding up your jockey shorts with a diaper pin; dining in fancy restaurants on credit cards that are perilously close to their credit limit (and you don't have even a cheap TV dinner in the fridge) -- this kind of insanity is the stuff that creates a class of people called "money slaves." They work but have nothing to show for it.

Maybe it doesn't bother a lot of people, but it bothers me. *A lot. As a matter of fact, it makes me mad as hell. There is absolutely no excuse for so many "working poor."*

The relentless pressure to spend is not fair to the worker. (Sure, the advertising industry has its hooks into *all of us* regardless of how much or little we earn!) *Dammit*, if you must work for a living you deserve to have something of real value to show for your time and effort. You deserve to keep part of everything you earn, and the opportunity *to make it work and grow for you.* It's an Orwellian form of slavery to work 40 or more hours a week for 40 years of your life and then have to worry about how you're going to pay for essentials, or if there will be enough to make life comfortable in your final years.

But not to worry. The government will take care of everybody. Or Social Security will take care of everybody. Or the company pension plan. Or . . . .

Anybody who believes the government, Social Security or a company pension will be enough to see them through their old age is not in touch with reality. The pitiful financial condition of a lot of current retirees trying to make ends meet on a mixture of government handouts, Social Security and a meager pension is proof that if you want to live with dignity you can't expect anyone else to take care of you. *You have to do it yourself.*

The good news is that you *can* do it. It will take knowing what you want, and wanting it badly enough to set short and long term goals that will get you where you're going. It will take plenty of guts, grit, determination and that unspeakably dirty word: *patience.* You will need a tough "*I can and will do it*" bulldog mentality that will enable you to go forward with your dreams and goals, and to succeed in achieving them, in spite of and regardless of what anybody else is doing or saying or urging you to do. You've got to *dare to be different*, to break free from "the pack." *Believe in yourself; believe in your ability to be the master of your money. You really can do it!*

You've got to start someplace. To help you get that start I am proposing two ways to beat "the system" that keeps us in financial bondage as perpetual motion money dispensing machines that put to shame the output of Las Vegas "one-armed bandits." The suggestions that follow are meant to be considered *in addition* to the recommendations made in other chapters.

YOUR PERSONAL LIFE

1. Look objectively at what is stealing every penny you earn. You also have to readjust your idea of what you need to be happy. It may take a lot of self-talk to convince yourself that you really can do without the things and people that are dragging you down. *But you can do it.*

2. *Be determined.* It's your life; it's your future. *Take charge of it!* If you are a procrastinator, please understand that the act of "putting things off until tomorrow" is the result of a choice you make. *You allow yourself to do it.* You have a free will; you can

make a conscious decision to do what you *know* you can and ought to be doing. Every day, ask yourself out loud: "Who is running *my life*, anyway?" If you don't lie to yourself and you don't like your answer, then change your behavior, attitude and environment until you can come up with an answer that you can live with. *Nobody is holding you back except you. Be your own best friend instead of your own worst enemy.* Some people will make sacrifices for strangers sooner than they will for themselves!

3. Stop being a "poor person." You stop being a "poor person" by taking X dollars from your next paycheck (before you spend a cent of it, even before paying bills!) and open a savings account. Take the same amount every month for six months. After the habit has been established, take a little more. Keep taking as much as you can, while looking for better, simpler, inexpensive ways to live and still have fun.

4. After you've figured out how much you can *realistically* save each payday, set some financial goals *and stick to them.*

5. Start educating yourself about money. You should be as smart about money as you are about the batting averages of your favorite sports figures. You should be able to talk with as much expertise about the intricacies of improving your financial condition as you do about the intimate details of Elvis Presley's "resurrection."

Taxes support the city library -- use it! There are

books, video tapes, magazines, financial newspapers and
newsletters that will open up a whole new and exciting
world to you. And don't forget your local bookstore.
They all carry a tremendous selection of self-help books
for serious wealth builders. As just one example, look
for Harold Moe's easy-to-read little gem titled *Make
Your Paycheck Last*. And be sure to buy the workbook
that goes with it. If you can't find it in a bookstore,
order directly from the publisher, Harsand Press, P.O.
Box 515, Holmen, WI 54636.

What kind of money management courses are being
offered at your local community college? Sign up for
one of them. If possible, get friends or co-workers to
sign up with you. Don't begrudge the time it will take.
It'll be far more beneficial than wasting the time
hanging out at the mall or the local saloon. As a bonus
you may get lucky and find a serious minded
"significant other" you've been dreaming about meeting.

6. Start talking "money" to co-workers and friends
who might become the nucleus of a support group.
What are their dreams and aspirations? But a word of
caution: Because the last thing you need is to be
laughed at or discouraged, don't tell them the details
of what you're planning or doing unless they show a
sincere interest in doing the same. Then and only then
ask them to join you with their own plan. You'll know
you've started a revolution and established yourself as a
leader when one-upmanship bull sessions around the

office water cooler turn from how much you all owe on your credit cards or the "really neat" status thing you just bought but don't need, to how much money you've *really* saved out of last week's paycheck.

7. Start talking with financial planners. (They're in the phone book.) Talk to a lot of them. The more you talk with them the more you'll learn, and you'll get a clearer picture of what you can really do with your money. If you find one with whom you think you can develop a good rapport, be honest with him or her. Admit you are starting with nothing. You'll know she's not totally motivated by greed if she agrees to nurse you along your path to prosperity. As you make money she'll make more money, and that's great. Nothing beats a win-win relationship.

8. Examine critically and "talk back" to advertising of all kinds and let those messages know *you absolutely positively will no longer respond to Pavlovian manipulation or emotional appeals that insult your intelligence.* You'll find that when you can deal with advertising analytically and with a clear understanding of what it's really all about, you'll actually *enjoy* it as an art form. It takes talent to convince the public to buy and eat the turtle turds dished up at the local Heave-Ho Burger Barge -- "fast food" that sinks like a lead anchor in your stomach and stays there growing barnacles for at least a week. It takes *a whole lot* of talent (and nerve) to make a deodorant commercial that

can sell the *hope* of finding romance and at the same time, chip away at your self-confidence by intimating that unless you buy and use the product you may offend people with body odor. And it certainly takes talent to convince beer drinkers that sex is waiting for them in a six-pack. By all means, appreciate and enjoy the talent and creativity that go into the production of advertising. And then thumb your nose at the message. Awareness of the *intent* of advertising puts *you* in charge of your pocketbook and can be exceedingly satisfying. When you can develop that degree of "smarts," then you'll buy what *you* need and want and *only* when *you* want it.

Life is a blast all by itself. You don't need to clutter it up with a lot of unnecessary consumer products that will make you sick, soon be forgotten, thrown away or stored in the attic for your heirs who won't appreciate your "treasures." They'd much prefer that you leave them money. *A lot of it.*

9. Be prepared to "backslide." Everybody does. By "backsliding" I mean there will be times you will be *very* tempted to throw in the towel. There will surely be *something* that you absolutely *must buy* that's more important than adding to your investment program, particularly if you are the impatient type and you don't think you are making enough progress. You may even be strongly tempted to "cash in your chips." *Resist the temptation, brothers and sisters! Amen?* Amen indeed!

Think long and hard before you allow your future prosperity to go down the drain. But here's the good news: Winners pick themselves up and start again -- as often as it takes. *And you are a winner!* Remember, it's determination and perseverance that will get you where you are going. And remember also, your twenties, thirties and forties are your miracle wealth-building years. Don't let them slip away from you without having something of value to show for having lived and worked through them.

Here's the bad news. If it were easy to start and maintain an investment plan, *everybody*, -- well, *nearly everybody*, would be doing it. It would become America's number one indoor sport.

The truth is, *it's tough. Real tough.* I've said it before and I'll say it again because it needs to be drummed into our minds until we can recognize and combat this reality: From early on we are conditioned to accept and respond to peer pressure; to do what everybody else is doing. (Out for dinner? Don't the gals go to the ladies room *together?*) On top of that, "going shopping" (meaning, spending money for the sake of spending money) *is where it's at.* Everybody does it; you don't even need cash to do it. It's a socially and politically approved national pastime deeply ingrained in a work and spend culture, -- the creation of an advertising industry that has been paid by businesses of all sizes, domestic and foreign, to sell their products --

that manipulates us unmercifully and wipes us out financially. It's a wonder so many of us avoid bankruptcy as well as we do.

Yes, saving money is *very tough.* And that takes us to the second way that workers can be helped to be financially independent at retirement and before.

CORPORATE INVOLVEMENT

Corporations spend a lot of money on self-serving activities designed to get good publicity or a tax break. There's nothing wrong with that. But sometimes, money given to some causes could be put to better use. Such as hiring an in-house financial planner to start employees on their way to financial independence.

It's really crazy. You give the best days of your life to one or more companies and when it's all over you don't have a hell of a lot to show for your *investment* of time, energy and effort. In many cases, there is *nothing.* Not even a gold watch or a rocking chair to show that you ever left the house every working day for the past 40 years.

Yes, you are making an *investment.* You have a limited number of hours and days on this earth. You get just one shot at making a wise investment of your time, talent and energy. So what you do with each and every day *is* an investment, be it good or bad.

The company you work for is making an investment,

too. It's investing and re-investing the profits produced by your labor. But as a rank and file worker you don't get "residuals," "commissions," or "dividends" on the profit you helped to generate.

The entertainment industry has finally come to grips with the recognition that a performer's time, talent and effort in the production of a movie or TV program is an investment. Yes, she gets paid for her work, but her contract also provides that as long as someone is profiting from the showing of her original investment of time, talent and effort, she is to share in the profits. Should the time, talent and effort of a lowly corporate worker be of any less significance or value? The idea bears repeating: The profit you helped to generate during your term of employment has been turned over, again and again, to produce even more profit for the company. There's nothing wrong with that. That's what makes the system work. But when you don't benefit accordingly -- that's *very* wrong!

Because it is impossible to judge just how much profit has been generated over a period of time by the talent, time and effort of an individual worker, no one would argue that workers are entitled to "residuals" or "commissions" on company investments. (On second thought, maybe that's not such a bad idea!) But how about entitlement to the services of a company financial planner?

The point of this celebrity-worker comparison is

that the system is *so damned lopsided*, particularly when employees wind up on the short end of the stick. There needs to be more *balance and fairness* in how workers are compensated for their time, talent and effort. *We're talking about human beings. We're talking about three to four decades of your life. We're talking about the best days of your life. Why aren't we expecting and asking for more than what most of us are getting in exchange for those precious hours, days and years?* Why aren't we getting financial planning assistance? Yes, we're being repetitious about the financial planning issue, but perhaps now is the time to get used to the idea that we may have to be *very* repetitious when trying to enlighten employers about providing help.

Corporate pride in running a "mean and lean" operation while neglecting the long-term welfare of employees reflects the notion that it's good management to take care of "Number One" and to hell with what's happening to anybody else. It's a niggardliness born of greed, devoid of compassion and responsibility and is ultimately destructive not just to the individual or entity that holds the view, but to society as a whole. It must be replaced with a new ethic rooted in generosity and caring *freely given*. It's not too much to expect or ask of those to whom we give the best days of our lives.

Note well that the emphasis is on help *freely given*.

This is not an argument for compulsion; just compassion. It cannot be over-emphasized: *Employees are human beings, not just perpetual motion machines to generate profit and keep money in circulation.*

Realistically, few companies will get off their myopic corporate duffs and do anything more for workers than they absolutely have to unless pushed, shoved and possibly shamed into it. In other words, the ball is in *your* court. Utilizing suggestions in previous chapters, get a committee together and tell your company and/or union leadership that *all of you want to be helped to have your share of the American Dream.* Our economic system is designed to allow everybody to prosper. *You deserve an opportunity to participate and share in it!* Remind them that until something better comes along, it's *the workers* who make things happen.

Listen, I *really do* care about what happens to you. You say I don't even know you? *But I do.* Every day that you go to work and must put up with an employer who only cares about how much productivity can be wrung out of you -- an employer that expects you to go the extra mile, but won't go the extra mile for you; and every time you are besieged with messages to throw away your money -- believe me, *I do know you.* And for the same reasons, *you know me.* I care about you because I don't like to see decent hard-working people constantly getting the shaft from so many sides and in so many ways. I care about you because unless you and a whole lot of other people are self-sufficient at least by retirement, the standard of living *of all of us* will be slashed significantly. *You* deserve better. *I* deserve better. *We* all deserve better. *You better believe I care!*

Life is not a rehearsal. When we get to the end of our own personal drama, either it has a happy ending or it doesn't. Fortunately, we are given the gift of a limited period of time in which we can work miracles. But no one forces us to take advantage of that gift. It's entirely up to each of us to use it profitably.

THE LAST WORD AND AN INVITATION

I am aware that what I am proposing and promoting may be considered "too simplistic" "too altruistic" "not do-able" or "not whatever" by statists, "experts," those educated beyond their intelligence and those with financial interests to protect (it's true -- a lot of people profit from other people's misfortune and poverty). But it's okay to be told you're crazy. History is filled with examples of progressive ideas shot down by men and women with little minds and selfish motives. Many of those unique ideas were worth fighting for, such as those finally brought to fruition in our Constitution for our everlasting benefit. For that major miracle we can thank those who loved freedom and cared enough about their fellow human beings and future generations to work, sacrifice and die for what they believed in.

Maybe helping workers to become financially secure is "not do-able." But we won't know unless we try, will we? Shucks, you and I know that Americans can do *anything* they decide they want to do. As a nation we started with an "impossible dream" of our Founding Fathers and we continue to perform major miracles every day. *Didn't we get to the moon?*

Be generous in discussing the ideas in this book, particularly with those who may not be able or inclined to read. Until put on audio tape, the thoughts expressed in these pages may not be available to them. These folks may become strong allies in your effort to improve your financial destiny. Remember, when we help others get what they need, we help ourselves.

Now, the invitation: There *are* companies with enlightened management doing a lot to help employees help themselves. Such companies should be recognized and encouraged. Are you working for and being helped by such a progressive company? Please write and tell me about it. My address is P.O. Box 6099, Oceanside, CA 92056. With your input perhaps a giant step can be taken to help *all* workers maximize their financial potential so that at retirement or before, we can *all* have more than we ever dared to dream possible.

INDEX

CLIP AND MAIL TODAY

		Quantity	Unit Price	Total
Minimum Wage to	Hardbound		$19.95	
Maximum Wealth	Softcover		$14.95	
			SUBTOTAL	
		CA residents add 7% sales		
		SHIPPING - Add $1.75 per copy		
			TOTAL	

SHIP TO:

Name _____

Address _____

City _____ State _____ Zip _____

Phone No. ( )
PLEASE INCLUDE

ALLOW 2 to 3 WEEKS FOR DELIVERY

MAIL TO:
TANGIBLE ASSETS
PUBLICATIONS
P.O. BOX 6099
OCEANSIDE, CA 92056